Microsoft Word 2007 for Beginners

Doug and Robin Hewitt

Champion Writers

Atlanta – Beijing – Harbin – Washington

Microsoft Word 2007 for Beginners
First Edition
Copyright © 2009 by Doug and Robin Hewitt

International Standard Book Number:
ISBN-13: 978-1-60830-018-1
ISBN-10: 1-60830-018-8

Printed in the United States of America.

Disclaimer
The author of this book is not affiliated with any software maker and/or its affiliates. Therefore, the views and opinions expressed in this book do not represent the views and opinions of any software maker and/or its affiliates.

The information presented in this book is for reference only. The author(s) and publisher strive to provide accurate information. Several factors will create different user experiences than the one presented in this book. These factors include variations of software versions, patches, operating systems, configurations, and customizations. This book is not warranted to be error-free or up-to-date.

Reference resources listed in this book, such as website addresses, may have changed after this book was published.

The author(s) and the publisher shall have neither liability nor responsibility to any person or entity with respect to any loss or damages arising from the information contained in this publication.

We Love to Hear from You!

Every reader of this book has something to say that we may learn from. Your opinions and comments are invaluable to us. While every precaution has been taken in the preparation of this book, there remains the possibility that errors or omissions still exist. If you find errors or omissions in this book, please check out the publisher's website and review all documented errata. If you do not find your issue on that list, please submit your comments to us, and we will update our website and correct all of the known issues in the next release.

Please note that the author(s) is unable to help you with any technical issues related to the topics included in this book. Due to the volume of messages we receive from our readers, we are unable to respond to every message; however, please be assured that your message will be carefully read, considered, and provided with a response when warranted.

When contacting us, please visit publisher's website at:

http://www.championwriters.com

Contents at a Glance

Table of Contents

Introduction

Why we're here

If you've looked through the shelves at your local bookstore for books that help people learn and use Microsoft Word 2007 (like we have), your heart might have sunk when you picked them and gazed at the number of pages between the covers of these massive tomes. Hundreds and hundreds of pages of detailed instruction greet you. For some books, the page count approaches 1,000!

What about people who simply want to learn the basics, to put together a family newsletter? Or maybe a letter to a loved one? Let's consider others, let's say college students, who need to learn how to use Microsoft Word 2007 in order to write term papers and the occasional letter home to ask for a few extra dollars to make it through till the next semester scholarship disbursement. We can think of other situations in which a Word user simply wants to accomplish a simple task or two and don't want to delve into dense instructional text to find out how to do them. For example, there are parents who would like to write letters of recommendation for school or employment. Sometimes, too, an official printed letter needs to be mailed to comply with legal requirements.

We wanted to write a book for true beginners, one that didn't intimidate readers with small text and thousands of topics. And at the same time, we thought we could write such a book and try to be mildly entertaining as well. We come at this as writers and readers, not computer programmers, and so we can appreciate good wording. While we admire people who can decipher new computer applications without so much as opening the user's manual, we think the user's manual should be enjoyable enough to read on its own merits.

Icons

As we walk you through the world of Microsoft Word 2007, there'll be times when we want to draw your attention to something that relates to what we're discussing or maybe something that's off topic but important enough to bring it up.

For these kind of information tidbits (we're tempted to call them bytes), we'll use icons to draw your attention to them. We'll use different icons for different types of information.

 topics about computers and their operation

 security topics (passwords, login IDs, etc)

 useful tips to note somewhere for later reference

 a point we want to make

 repair mistakes (we all make them)

 warnings and alerts

Other Conventions

We'll try to use as many screenshots as possible to help you visually understand what we're talking about. A screenshot is a picture of our computer screen. It's what we're looking at as we write this book.

Also, we'll also be telling you to select certain commands. We'll get into how that's done (selecting a command) in a moment, but for now all you need to know is that the Word 2007 menu commands will be in **bold**. So, for example, we might tell you to select the **Print** command. **Print** would be an option that we want you to select with your mouse.

Sometimes we'll use words in italics. Words in italics can be:

- *web addresses* (URLs, pronounced you are ells)
- *words we want to stress* (like in the bullet above)
- *book titles*
- *program names*
- *path names* (don't worry, we'll explain later)
- *file names*

A Sneak Peek

As we already mentioned, we'll be putting in screenshots of what you'll be looking at with your Word 2007 screen. With that in mind, we'll jump ahead and give you a sneak peak at the first screenshot.

When you open Microsoft Word 2007, you'll see a screen that already has a new document opened. In a way, you're already in gear and can start typing text.

First, though, if you're unfamiliar with how to open Word, we're here to help. The steps to open Word 2007 depends on the type of operating system you have. Most personal computers run on a Microsoft operating system (OS, pronounced Oh *Ess*, is how tech-savvy people refer to it), and we'll describe the steps for the Microsoft OS. If you have something else, check with your computer's documentation.

Introduction

 When we tell you to press the left mouse button, we'll be shortening this to "*left click*" on something.

- Move your mouse to point the cursor at the **Start** button, usually in the lower left corner on your computer monitor.
- Press the left mouse button with the pointer over the **Start** button to select it.
- Left click on **All Programs.**
- Use the scroll bar to scroll through the programs until you find the Microsoft Office folder.
- Left click on the folder.
- Left click on **Microsoft Word 2007**.

Now, wasn't that easy?

You're on your way to using Word.

The first area in the Word layout we want to direct your attention to is the button in the upper left corner. While the **Start** button is in the lower left corner, when you have Word 2007 open, there's a button in the upper left corner. This button is called the **Office Button**. You need to know this button because it's where you'll save your work.

 The **Office Button**

Left click on the Office Button and you're presented with a dialog box.

As you can see, you're presented with a series of command options. We'll go through some of those commands in the next chapter. For now, congratulations. You're on your way to using Microsoft Word 2007.

Summary

We introduced ourselves and our goals in writing this book, making it useful for beginners. We explained some of the icons we'll be using in this book, and when we'll use **bold** and italics text.

We've shown you how to open Microsoft Word 2007 and where the **Office Button** is located. As we move ahead, we'll learn that for beginners, the Office Button is the key to getting started and also for saving your work.

CHAPTER 1

Creating and Saving Word Documents

Introduction

We're going to show you how to create Word files and then save them. Why would you want to save a Word file? You might want to modify it later or print it later. Or you just might want to save it for your personal records. This is important if it's an official document, such as correspondence to the I.R.S. The point is, if you don't save it, it'll be gone.

Saving is one thing, *finding* is another.

It's important to understand that you need to be able to find your Word file after you save it. We'll give you a few tips on good locations, such as your computer desktop. Once you know how to create and save files, you'll have the basis for returning to your work, whether it's the next day or the next week.

Create a New Document

Let's get started! We're going to show you how to create a new document. Later, we're going to save and print it.

1) Open *Microsoft Word 2007.*

2)   Left click on the **Office Button**.
3)   Left click on the **New** command.

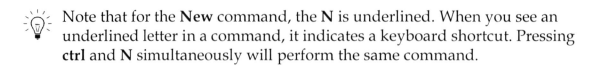 Note that for the **New** command, the **N** is underlined. When you see an underlined letter in a command, it indicates a keyboard shortcut. Pressing **ctrl** and **N** simultaneously will perform the same command.

You're now presented with a New Document dialog box.

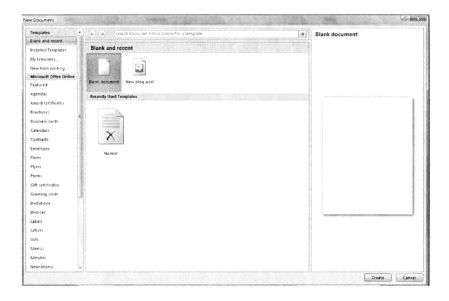

4)   Select **Blank document** by left clicking on it.
5)   Left click on the **Create** button.

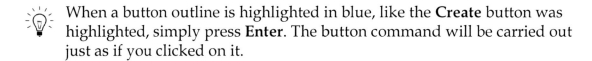 When a button outline is highlighted in blue, like the **Create** button was highlighted, simply press **Enter**. The button command will be carried out just as if you clicked on it.

New Document Screen Features

You'll notice a lot of different icons and words and settings in the top section of your computer monitor. All of these commands can be frightening to beginners,

Creating and Saving Word Documents

who often ask the question, Where do I start?

Let's look at the main features of your Word user interface. That's what it is, after all, an interface. It's the mechanism, the means, by which you interact with the Word document. It displays information for you to read and presents commands for you to give.

We'll list the main features, give a description, and show you where these features are located on the screen.

Document Name	This tells you your document name is Document1 (an indication you haven't given it a name yet). If you created another document, it would automatically be given the name *Document2*. In our example, our document title is *Word 2007 for Beginners Chapter 1*.
Tabs	Below the document name is a row of words. These are called the *Tabs*. Left clicking on a tab gives you a choice of commands related to that tab. The tabs you'll see here are: **Home, Insert, Page Layout, References, Mailings, Review**, and **View**.
Ribbon	The Ribbon is a row directly below the tabs. In the Ribbon, functions and commands are displayed such as **Paste** and **Format Painter**. These commands are grouped together in Groups.
Group	Each group of commands is named at the bottom of the Group. The Groups you'll see on your opening screen are *Clipboard, Font, Paragraph, Styles*, and *Editing*. Each *Group* is separated by a border of a slightly different shade of color.

Launcher	Most, but not all, *Groups* have a small square button at the bottom right of each *group's* border. This is called the *Launcher*. Left clicking the Launcher will open a dialog box with more related commands.
Help	At the far right side of the row of *Tabs* is a small circle with a question mark in it. Left clicking this will launch *Word Help*.
Quick Access Toolbar	Above the row of tabs, near the Office Button, are a couple of icons for Save, Undo, and Redo. This area is the Quick Access Toolbar. You can add commands that you frequently use to this area.
Office Button	Left clicking the **Office Button** will open a dialog box with commands related to the file with which you're working such as **Print** and **Save**. Word Options is also accessed through the **Office Button.**

Using Your Mouse

Because you've opened a new document, there's nothing in it yet. This means that your insertion point, which is a blinking vertical bar, will appear only in the upper left corner of your document.

As you move your mouse pointer around the screen, you'll notice that it changes shape, depending on where it's at on the screen. If you're pointing at the document and are within the margins, you'll see it change to a figure resembling an I-Beam.

This is the tool you can use to change your insertion point. As you fill up your document with words, you'll be able to left click the I-Beam into different parts of the document where you want to insert words, change text, and work with your document.

If you move your cursor into the left margin, the cursor will change into an arrow. This is your *Selection Tool* and we'll be using it later to select portions of text.

Write Your Document

We're going to begin with a simple two-paragraph resume letter. This could be a letter that you send along with your resume when you're applying for a job. The commands we'll show you in creating and saving your cover letter will be the foundation on which you'll soon be a whiz with Word. We'll also show you a few basic formatting commands.

To write your document:

1) Write your name and address, hitting **enter** at the end of each line.
2) Press **enter** again to add space below your name and address.
3) Write your salutation, *"Dear Human Resources Manager,"*.
4) Press **enter** again to add space below your salutation.
5) Write your opening paragraph.
6) Press **enter** to add space below your first paragraph.
7) Write your second paragraph.
8) Press **enter** to add space after your second paragraph.
9) Write your closing line.
10) Press **enter**.
11) Write *"Sincerely,"*.
12) Press **enter** twice so you'll room to write your name with a pen.
13) Type your name.

Congratulations! You've written your first document. It should look similar to the one we wrote.

Of course there's a much easier way to add space after your paragraphs, and we'll show you this setting later. Also, you might have noticed as you were writing your paragraphs that when your typing reached the right side of the document, the words automatically shifted to the next line. This is called word wrapping. Word wrapping will vary with your margin settings.

Now the next thing you need to do is save your document so you don't lose it.

Save Your Document

You can save your document at any point when you're working on it. You don't have to wait until you're finished. In fact, it's wise to save your work often so you don't lose it in the case of a computer crash. Word has an **Autosave** function, and we'll show you how to set that later. For now, we're going in and manually saving our resume letter.

A quick note first about why we're going to select the **Save As** command instead of the Save command. There are two reasons. One, when you select **Save As**, you'll be able to see the folder in which you're saving your document. It's always good to know where your documents are saved, and later we'll show you how to have multiple locations to save your documents.

The second reason is that Microsoft Word 2007 saves documents in a format that has a .docx extension. These are the letters that appear after your file name and describes the type of file it is. Word 2003 saves files with a .doc extension. The problem is, if you're sending your document to someone who uses Word 2003, they won't be able to open your document if it has a .docx extension.

So, just to play it safe for now, we're going to select Word 2003 in the **Save As** command.

To save your document:

1) Left click on the **Office Button**.
2) Move your pointer over the **Save As** command. A dialog box will appear.

3) Left click on the **Word 97-2003 command**. Another dialog box will appear.

Move your cursor into the *file name* box and left click. There will be a default name such as *doc1 or doc3*. In our case, Word 2007 looks at the document and suggests a name based on the opening line, *Jill or John Q*. Delete these letters by hitting backspace or highlighting the name and pressing **delete**. Type in the name of your file. For ours, we typed in *Resume Letter 1*.

Select the location of where you're going to save your file. You'll notice there is a bar with **Organize, Views**, and **New Folder**. Below this bar there are two boxes. The box to the left is titled *Folders* and the box to the right lists the documents in the folder selected on the left.

If you're familiar with *Folders*, find the folder you want to work with, such as *My Folders,* and left click on it. Otherwise, we're going to save our file to the *Desktop*, which is an icon in the Folders box on the left. Left click on *Desktop*, then left click on **Save**.

Close Your Document

Let's say you're finished working and want to turn off your computer. Maybe you have a laptop and are getting ready to head off to school.

There are a couple of ways to close out.

The easiest? Left click on the *red* X button in the upper right corner. An easy way to remember this command it that it's the *eXit* button.

This is a good time to explain the other commands with the mini-toolbar. They are **Minimize** and maximize commands. They change the way Word is displayed onscreen. The **Minimize** button will collapse the Word application to a button in the *Taskbar*. The *Taskbar* is the bar at the bottom of your screen, where the *Start* button is located.

 The button on the left is **Minimize**. The middle button is **Maximize**. The *red* **X** button is the *eXit* button.

The other way to close out your document is to left click on the Office Button. Then select **Close** or **Exit Word**. If you choose Close, the Word 2007 application will remain active, but your document will close. Choosing Exit Word will close the document and the application.

Go ahead and close out by whichever method appeals to you.

Open Your Document

Now, open Word 2007 like you did previously, from the Start button.

> 1) After Word is open, left click on the **Office Button.**
> 2) Select **Open**.
> 3) Left click on the *Folder* box and select *Desktop*.

Find your document in the box to the right. You might have to scroll down by using the scroll bar. Just lift click on the scrolling button and drag it down. Once you find your document, left click on the name to select it.

    4) Click **Open**.

 Write down the name of your files with a pen on a notepad with a brief description of the contents. A date could be helpful, too.

Print Your Document

We're going to assume you have a printer hooked up to your computer. If you don't, connecting your printer to your computer is beyond the scope of this beginner's book. And whenever something is beyond the scope of a book, that means ask your computer-savvy friends for help. Some computer stores will assist you in setting up your printer if you buy one from them.

For now, let's assume your printer has already been connected to your computer. Now, with your document opened, it's in mint-perfect shape to be printed and mailed off with your resume. We'll show you how to make text changes later. For now, it's mint-perfect.

To print your document:

    1) Left click the **Office Button**.
    2) Move your pointer over the **Print** command. A dialog box opens.
    3) Left click on **Print** in the new dialog box.
    4) Left click on **OK**.

You should now have a printed resume letter. Go ahead and close out your document and exit Word. Check your printed page in the printer paper tray. You'll want to make sure it looks ok. After all, your printer might be out of ink!

Chapter Summary

In this chapter we showed you how to create a new document in Word 2007.

Creating and Saving Word Documents

We typed some basic text, creating a letter. Then we saved this as a file on our computer desktop.

We then closed the file and re-opened it. We showed you how to name the file and how to print it.

These are very basic steps at this point. Word 2007 is a very powerful application with a gazillion commands. We're not going to overwhelm you, at least not initially. As we progress to later chapters, we'll start listing more and more commands in table form and tell you what each command does. By that time, you'll be more familiar with Word 2007 and it should make more sense to you at that time than if we list dozens of commands early on in this book.

CHAPTER 2

Working with Text

Introduction

Now that we've shown you how to create documents and save them on your computer, along with typing in some simple text, we're going to show you how to work with text in this chapter. For example, you might want more spacing between the lines of your text. Or you might want to have a sentence or maybe just one word in **bold** or *italics*.

Word 2007 is a powerful word processing application, and we could devote an entire book on working with text. But that's not what we're here for. We're here to show you the basics. Once you're comfortable with working with the basics, and you get comfortable using the basic Word 2007 *Tabs* and *Commands*, you can explore the other Groups in the Ribbon if you have the inclination.

So let's get on with some simple lessons on working with text.

Fonts

A font is a typeface. It's a style of how the letters look, the shape of them. Word 2007 has numerous fonts that you can work with. Let's take a look and see what kind of fonts you might want to try.

Chapter 2

- Open Word 2007 and then open a new document.
- Take a look at the *Font* group in the Ribbon bar.

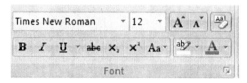

This is the *Font* group. It's under the *Home* tab. You can select commands in this group to change the appearance of your words.

For our version of Microsoft Word 2007, we have *Times New Roman* as the default font. Click on the downward pointing arrowhead beside the words "Time New Roman" and a dialog box appears. This is the list of fonts that you currently have installed. Note there is a scroll bar in the dialog box. Scroll down to see more available fonts.

We're going to select a font called Calibri and type a few paragraphs of text.

Let's have a little fun while we're learning about Word 2007. Let's say you're writing your first essay for school. Try to write three paragraphs for your essay. Include a title and a byline.

Here's our example.

Figure 2-1

If you're sending your file to someone using a different computer with another word processing application, they might not have some of the more exotic fonts. Times New Roman and Ariel are always safe bets to use in your documents. Calibri isn't a bad choice, either.

It's important to note the sequence here of what we did. Before we typed our text, we selected a font. Afterward, every word we typed was in the font we selected. That's not the only way to select a font for text. We'll show you the second way.

Changing Text Font

Now that we have some text in Calibri, we're going to change some of the text to a different font. We're not going to change all of our text, just one paragraph. Let's have some fun. We're not sending this to anyone else, someone who might not have an exotic font on their computer, so let's select a font that simply looks cool.

But first, we have to select text. Maybe we only want to change the font of the second paragraph.

To select text:

1) Move your pointer arrow over the text. It will become an I-beam cursor (vertical line with half-curls at the top and bottom).
2) Move the I-beam cursor to the front of the first letter of the first word of the text you want to select.
3) Press the left mouse button and keep it pressed.
4) Use the mouse to move the I-beam to just behind the last letter or character (such as the period of a sentence) of the text you want to select.
5) Release the left mouse button.

There is another way to select text if you're going to select an entire line or paragraph of text. You can also select multiple paragraphs. We're spending a lot of time talking about selecting text because these methods are important to making the changes you want to make to your text and essay.

To select a line or paragraph or multiple paragraphs:

1) Move your pointer arrow to the left of the text, making sure it is a pointer and not an I-beam. Align the point of the arrow with the first line of text you want to select.
2) Press the left mouse button and keep it pressed.
3) Use the mouse to move the pointer up or down. Entire lines of text will become highlighted as you move your pointer.
4) When all of the lines of text you want are selected, release the left mouse button.

 If you make a mistake and select the wrong text, simply click the mouse pointer (as an I-beam) anywhere in the document, and your text will be de-selected.

Now that you have the text selected, move your mouse pointer to the Font group. Use the font drop-down dialog box to select a different font. When you select a different font, the highlighted text will change to the font you've selected. We've selected a new font for us, *Segoe Script*.

As you can see, we haven't really Here's the start of our second paragraph, which is now with a *Segeo Script* font.

Okay, one last point on selecting text.

This is important!

Click anywhere in your document when your pointer is an I-beam.
Press down the **cntl** key on the keyboard, otherwise known as the control key. While you have the **cntl** key pressed, briefly press the **A** key. Release both keys at the same time.

Wa la! You've selected all of the text in your document.

- **Cntl** + **A** = *select all text in the document.*

This is what's known as a *keyboard shortcut*. We won't be covering many in the book, less than half a dozen. So when we do take the time to show you one, you can be sure that we think you're going to want to use it somewhere down the road.

 Use a 3x5 index card to write down keyboard shortcuts for easy reference later.

Mini Toolbar

You might have noticed a new feature for Word 2007. It's called a Mini Toolbar. It pops up whenever you select text. It's a convenient way to change some of the basic text properties such as the font. In our previous example with the English essay paper, we went to the *Font* group with our mouse pointer and made our changes via the group commands.

Instead, you can use the Mini Toolbar commands.
The Mini toolbar is a neat new feature of Word 2007. It appears whenever you select text and has the same commands (mostly) that reside in the *Font* group up in the *Ribbon*.

We've selected some text in our essay and will show you the Mini Toolbar that we see as we work with our document.

Figure 2-2

In Figure 2-2, you can see some of our second paragraph with the *Segoe Script* font. You can also see some of the third paragraph, which we've selected (and so it's highlighted with a background color). Because we've selected text, namely, the third paragraph, the Mini Toolbar has popped up on our screen.

We're going to go over the commands in the *Font* group, though. Just be aware that these commands are also available in the Mini Toolbar. Use the Mini Toolbar buttons or the buttons in the *Font* group. Use whichever method you're most comfortable with.

If you want to save your new document, your *First Class Essay*, now's the time!

Turning the Mini Tool Bar On and Off

Before we get into the format commands, and because we're focused on the Mini Toolbar, we're going to show you how to turn the Mini Toolbar on and off. To do this, we have to delve into the world of Word options. You can change all kinds of options in Word, from having your documents automatically spell-checked to changing the Command buttons on the Ribbon.

To turn the Mini Toolbar off (or on):

1) Click on the **Office Button**.
2) Click on the **Word Options** button. It's on the bottom bar of the dialog box. See below for what it looks like.

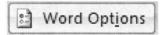 This is the **Word Options** *button* from the **Office Button** dialog box.

3. Click on the box beside the text "Show Mini Toolbar on selection." This will remove or insert the checkmark. It's like a toggle switch. Off and on. On and off.

Here's a picture of the Word Options dialog box. The very first command toggles the Mini Toolbar on and off. Can you find the checkmark box for the Mini Toolbar?

Figure 2-3

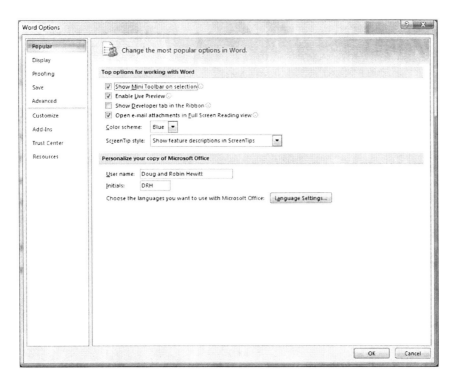

We'll return to the Word Options dialog box later. We wanted to introduce you to this important dialog box so that it will be familiar when we revisit it. And of course, we know some people might be distracted by the Mini Toolbar, so we wanted to show you how to turn it off.

For now, let's move on and look at how to do some basic text formatting.

Font Group Commands

Let's take another look at the *Font* group. If you don't see it in your Ribbon, you might have to select the Home tab. That's the tab under which the Font group resides.

We'll list these *Font* group commands in a table. How does it work? After you select text in your document, go to the *Font* group and click on a command. View your document to see how it changes the look of the words. After a while, you might develop an artistic flair for making your words look aesthetically pleasing on the page!

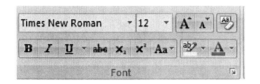 Here's another look at the *Font* group. Click on the *Home* tab is you don't see it.

Here's a table that lists the commands of the Font group. Play around with selecting text, then selecting a command to see how it changes the look of your text.

Times New Roman ▾	Change the font (also called the font face).
12 ▾	Change the size of the font.
A A	There are two buttons here. The first increases the size of the font. The second decreases the size of the font.
Aa (eraser icon)	Clears (also called erasing) all formatting of the selected text. This will leave only the formatting of the default plain text.
B	Makes the text **bold**.
I	Makes the text *italics*.
U	Makes the text <u>underlined</u>.
abc	Puts a ~~strikethrough~~ line through the text.
X_2	Makes the text a subscript, such as the number 2 in the molecular H_2O.
X^2	Makes the text a superscript such as the 2 in the equation $E=MC^2$.

Working with Text

Aa — Changes the case of the text. You can capitalize every letter, the first letter of each word, and so on. Click on the down-pointing arrowhead to see your choices.

ab — Make the text appear as though it was highlighted with a highlighting pen. You can select different colors of highlighting pens.

A — Change the color of the text.

Have you ever wondered why the size of the font is given in units called points? It's a term that comes from the days when printers used typesets. The term stuck.

 The point size is the size of your text. One inch equals 72 points.

Let's go back and look at our first class essay. In addition to some of the basic formatting commands available in the Font group, you might want to learn a few other basic commands in order to meet style guidelines for the essay.

There are three basic commands you need to know beyond the *Font* group commands.

They involve *justification*, which means your text is left or right justified (aligned with the left or right side of the page) or centered on the page.

Line spacing. Your English teacher might want your essay double spaced or single spaced. This is an important command to know.

Indent. Your teacher might want the first line of your paragraph indented. The typical indent is 0.5 inch. Because *Indent* is getting more in depth into the *Paragraph* group, we're going to save that for Chapter 3.

We'll show you where these commands are. We suggest opening your document *My First Class Essay* and making the changes to your text. We'll show you how our essay looked after the changes we made, which is how yours should look if you selected the commands correctly.

Justification

We want to center the title and byline of our *My First Class Essay*. To center your text, you need to know where the justification commands are. They're in the *Paragraph* group, which is just to the right of the Font group. Here's a picture of the *Paragraph* group.

 Here's a picture of the *Paragraph* group.

We're not going to delve into the numerous commands of the Paragraph group for the moment. There are, though, four buttons that serve as justification commands and one button that will change your line spacing. Here are the buttons and what commands they enforce.

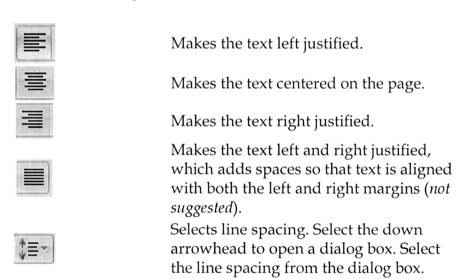

Makes the text left justified.

Makes the text centered on the page.

Makes the text right justified.

Makes the text left and right justified, which adds spaces so that text is aligned with both the left and right margins (*not suggested*).

Selects line spacing. Select the down arrowhead to open a dialog box. Select the line spacing from the dialog box.

Now, go to your essay. Do the following tasks.
Center your title and byline. Remember, select your text first. Select only the title

and byline. Then click on the "text centered" button.
Select the three paragraphs of the body of your essay.

Select single spacing from the line spacing dialog box.

Here's a picture of the *Line Spacing* dialog box. A checkmark appears beside your current selection. We've changed ours to *2.0*.

We selected double spacing, which is "2.0".

Note that your three paragraphs are still highlighted. Click anywhere on the page to remove the highlighting. Next chapter, we'll change the indent spacing of the first line of each paragraph.

Want to know what our *My First Class Essay* looks like? Here's a picture.

Figure 2-4

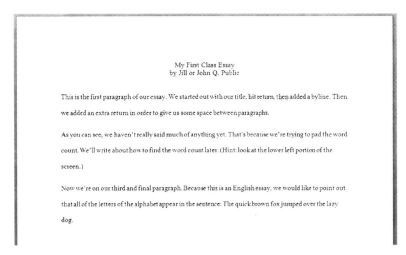

Conclusion

In this chapter, we've shown you how to select specific parts of your document. You can select a single word, a paragraph, or an entire document. We've also given you a keyboard shortcut to select the entire document.

Once you've selected text in your document, you can change the formatting properties of the selected text. You can do this via the commands in the *Font* group or in the Mini Toolbar. And we've promised to show you how to indent the first line of your paragraphs! That's in the next chapter, so read on!

CHAPTER 3

Working with Paragraphs

Introduction

We've shown you how to create documents and to work with text. By the end of this chapter, you should be getting a comfortable feeling about working with Word. As you proceed through the rest of this book, this feeling will grow into one of confidence. We haven't shown you a lot of fancy tricks in this book, but that's not what we're here for. We want you to feel comfortable with Word basics.

There are, though, some formatting commands for paragraphs that you need to know about if you're going to gain that confidence. We'll cover those *Paragraph* commands in this chapter. We're going to also throw in a few other commands that we most often use, commands that can save you a lot of time such as the **Undo** command.

We believe that once you're familiar with the commands in the first three chapters in this book, you'll be knowledgeable enough to write the most basic of documents. They might not be fancy, but you also might not need anything beyond the most basic of formats.

Word Help

We're going to show you where you can go for help for working with *Microsoft Word*

2007, other than this book, of course.

- Open *Microsoft Word 2007.*
- Open your file *My First Class Essay.*

Now, look in the upper right corner of your screen. You'll see a small button with a question mark in it. This is the **Word Help** button.

                    The **Word Help** button.

Click on the button and a dialog box appears.

Figure 3-1 Word Help Dialog Box

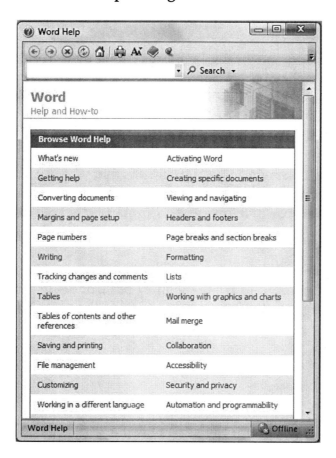

Simply type the topic into the white box and hit **enter**. You'll be shown instructions and explanations for the topic you entered. You can also click on the topics shown in the dialog box to access information on those topics.

 Type your topic in the form of a question, such as "how do I add page numbers" to help Word identify the best instructions for your specific need.

Quick Access Toolbar

You still have *My First Class Essay open*, right? Look at the upper left portion of your screen. Beside the Microsoft Button, you'll see a short row of command buttons. This is the *Quick Access Toolbar*. For now, we're going to show you the existing commands on this toolbar, but in a later chapter we'll show you how to add the commands that you use most frequently. Having your often used commands in one toolbar can definitely be a time-saver.

 The *Quick Access Toolbar.*

Let's see what each of these command buttons do.

 This is the **Save** button. If you've already saved your document once, it will save it with the same name and file format. If it's a new document and you haven't saved it yet, it opens the **Save As** dialog box so you give your document a name and select a file type.

 This is the **Undo** command. It reverses your latest action. If you accidently perform a command, select **Undo** to correct your mistake.

 This is the **Redo** (pronounced *re-dew*) command. If you made a mistake by selecting **Undo**, select **Redo** to repeat the action that you undid.

Try out the **Undo** and **Redo** buttons!

1. Select a word in *My First Class Essay*.
2. Delete the word.
3. Select **Undo**. Your word reappears as the deletion is reversed.
4. Select **Redo** to automatically perform the deletion again.
5. Select **Undo** one last time to get your deleted word back again.

The Paragraph Group

We've already gone over a few commands, those that are associated with the justification of text such as right justified or left justified, in the *Paragraph* group. Now we're ready to show you the rest.

 The *Paragraph* group. It's under the *Home* tab and is beside the *Font* Group.

First we'll explain each command; then we'll go into our document *My First Class Essay* and see how these commands work.

Paragraph **Group Commands**

Bullets. Starts a bulleted list. Select text first to create a bulleted list.

Numbering. Starts a numbered list. Select text first to create a numbered list.

Multilevel List. Starts a multilevel list.

Decrease Indent. Decreases the indent of the paragraph.

Increase Indent. Increases the indent of the paragraph.

Working with Paragraphs

 Sort. Sorts a list alphabetically or numerically.

 Show/Hide ¶. Toggles between showing and hiding formatting marks such as the paragraph mark (shown).

 These are the **Justification** buttons (left, right, centered, and left and right) that we covered in Chapter 2.

 Line Spacing. This button selects line spacing, which we explained in Chapter 2. Select the down arrowhead to open a dialog box. Select the line spacing from the dialog box.

 Shading. This puts a highlight color behind selected text.

 Borders. This is a borders and gridlines button. With this button, you can add borders to tables, view table gridlines, and open the **Borders and Shading** Dialog Box.

 Paragraph. Opens the *Paragraph* command dialog box.

Now, open your document *My First Class Essay* if you haven't already done so.

After the third paragraph, press **enter**, then type the following five lines.

> This is the first line in my list.
> This is the second line in my list.
> This is the third line.
> The fourth.
> The fifth and final line in my list.

Here is what your Word document should look like.

Figure 3-2 Five Text Lines for a List

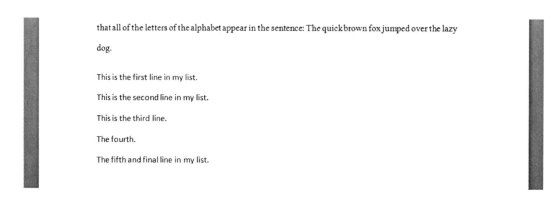

Select the five text lines (or, you could call them paragraphs because you pressed **enter** after each line). Your text becomes highlighted.

Figure 3-3 Selecting Your Five Text Lines

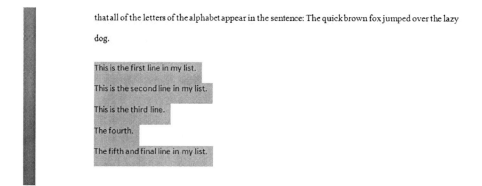

Now, select the **Bullets** command in the *Paragraph* group. Click your I-beam cursor somewhere in the document to de-select the text. Your page should now have a bulleted list.

Figure 3-4 Bulleted List

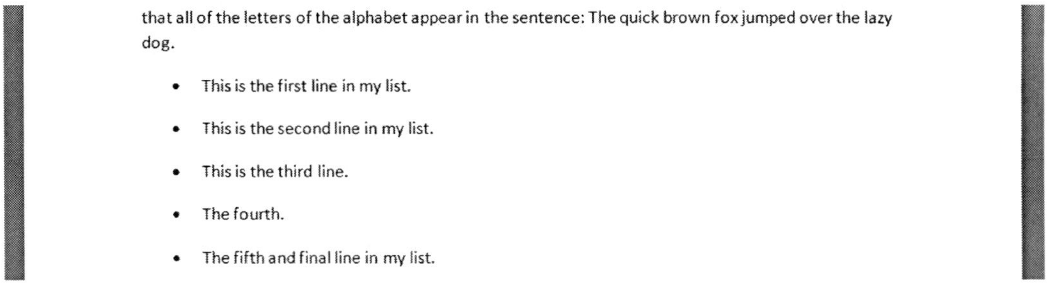

that all of the letters of the alphabet appear in the sentence: The quick brown fox jumped over the lazy dog.

- This is the first line in my list.
- This is the second line in my list.
- This is the third line.
- The fourth.
- The fifth and final line in my list.

Now, select the five lines again. Select **Numbering** in the *Paragraph* group. Click your I-beam cursor somewhere in the text to de-select the text. Your page should have a numbered list.

Figure 3-5 Numbered List

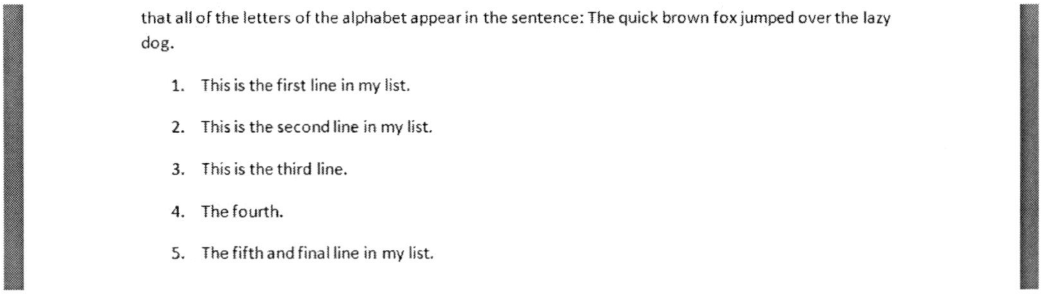

that all of the letters of the alphabet appear in the sentence: The quick brown fox jumped over the lazy dog.

1. This is the first line in my list.
2. This is the second line in my list.
3. This is the third line.
4. The fourth.
5. The fifth and final line in my list.

Now, let's say we want to center our list on the page and to bring the lines closer together in single line spacing. Easy! Select the five lines. Click on the **Center** button in the *Paragraph* group. Click on the downward arrowhead in the **Line Spacing** command button and select **1.0** for single spacing.

If you're following along, you'll notice that your lines might not be as close together as you'd expect for single spacing. That's because Word can add space automatically after a paragraph mark, or when your press **enter**.

Select the **Paragraph** command arrow in the bottom right corner of the *Paragraph* group. You'll see the following.

Figure 3-6 Spacing Commands in Paragraph dialog box

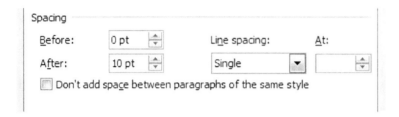

Note that the *Line Spacing* is set at *Single* because that's the result of our selection at the **Line Spacing** command button. But there is "*10 pt*" added after each of our paragraphs, or whenever we press **enter**. Select the downward facing arrowhead beside the "*10 pt*" and press twice to select "*0 pt*". Click on **OK**. Then click your I-beam cursor somewhere in the text to de-select the text.

Your list should now look like ours.

Figure 3-7 Numbered List, Centered

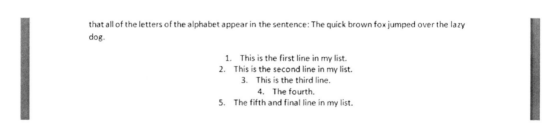

If you decide that you don't want your list to be a numbered list, select the lines of text and click on the **Numbering** command again.

We suggest clicking on the **Bullets** command and then the **Left Justify** command so that you can follow along with the changes we're making to our document as we write.

Paragraphs

What is a paragraph?

Many of us can remember some vague high school English definition of a set of sentences that are related to each other. For *Microsoft Word 2007*, it is useful to think of a paragraph as the lines of text the go before the paragraph mark symbol (and after the previous paragraph mark). The paragraph mark symbol looks like this: ¶.

Click on the **Show/Hide ¶** command (the button just has the paragraph mark symbol).

Your document will be dotted with paragraph mark symbols, one for every time you pressed **enter**.

Hide your paragraph mark symbols by clicking on the **Show/Hide ¶** again, noting that this commands acts like a toggle switch, turning the symbols on and off.

Paragraphs in *My First Class Essay*

We're going to make changes to all of the paragraphs in *My First Class Essay*. What we want to do is change all of the line spacing to single spacing with no extra space after the end of any of the paragraphs. We also want to indent the first line of each paragraph.

How do we make these changes? They're easy to do now that you understand how paragraphs appear in your document.

To make the paragraph changes:

1) Click your I-beam cursor in your document.
2) Press **ctrl** and **a** at the same time to "select all" of the text in your document (keyboard shortcut).
3) Click on the **Paragraph** command in the lower right corner of the *Paragraph* group. A dialog box appears.

Figure 3-8 Paragraph Dialog Box

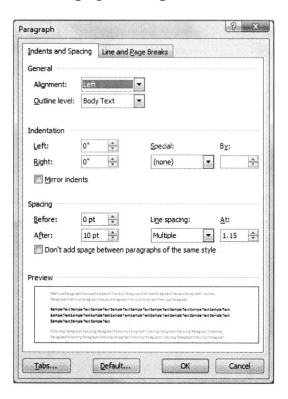

4) In the *Indentation* section, click on the down arrow under "*Special:*"
5) Select **First Line**. Notice the "*By:*" amount goes to 0.5 inches. That's a good indentation amount, but this is the place to change it if you later decide that a smaller or larger indentation is your preference.
6) Click on the down arrow under *Line Spacing:*
7) Select **Single**. Note that this is where to change line spacing in your document.

 Remember, the changes you make in the *Paragraph* dialog box will affect the selected text. If you open a new document, you can make these selections initially, then all of your text will follow the selected format.

8) Click on the selection arrows beside "*After:*" under *Line Spacing:* and select 0 pt.
9) Click on **OK**.

You might have noticed one particular feature of *Paragraph* dialog box, namely, the *Preview* pane. When you make a change in the *Paragraph* dialog box, going from double spacing to single spacing for example, the sample text in the *Preview* pane gives you a preview of the effect of your selection.

Figure 3-10 Preview Pane

Our document looks like the one below. Don't forget to click on **Save** to save your document. Remember, you can go back to your document, select different portions of text, and try different line spacing formats and different commands in the *Paragraph* dialog box. Practicing with Word commands will help you to locate them later, when you need them.

If you haven't centered your title and byline, select them in your *My First Class Essay* document, then click on **Center Justification**.

Figure 3-9 Single Spacing and Indented First Lines

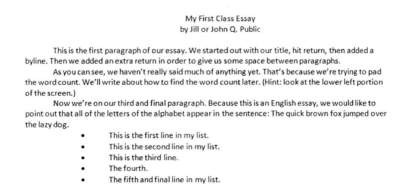

Paragraph Tidbits

We're going to save some of the commands in the Paragraph dialog box, which appears when you select the Paragraph command in the lower right corner of the Paragraph group, for later. The **Tabs** and **Default** commands are two of those. *Line and Page Breaks* is a tab selection that we'll also cover later.

Note that you can increase (and decrease) the indention of the lines of text. Simple click on the increase and decrease arrows in the *Indentation* section.

Indentation section. Increase and decrease the left and right margins here.

These perform the same functions as the **Decrease Indent** and **Increase Indent** command buttons in the Paragraph group.

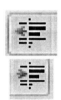

Decrease Indent. Decreases the indent of the paragraph.

Increase Indent. Increases the indent of the paragraph.

Other commands that we haven't covered in the *Paragraph* group in this chapter include **Multilevel List**, **Sort**, **Shading**, and **Borders**. If you're feeling adventurous, you can click on **Word Help** and type the command into the search window. Read about the command and practice using it on your document.

Conclusion

This chapter focused on the paragraph. We covered commands in the *Paragraph* group, and also the commands that are available when the *Paragraph* dialog box is opened via the **Paragraph** command. These commands included those that change the way your text appears in a document, including line spacing, indentation, and margins. We showed you how to indent the first line of every paragraph.

We also covered bulleted lists and numbered lists in this chapter. These lists are great ways for your documents to have a better visual impact.

The *Quick Access Toolbar* was covered in this chapter, including the **Undo** and **Redo** commands. Remember, **Undo** is an essential command for correcting mistakes. The word has crept into our vocabulary. In our daily lives, we are always looking to *undo* our errors.

It might be useful at this point to review the commands in the first three chapters of this book. Once you know the commands in these chapters, you'll be able to create, open, and save documents. You'll be able to change the font and the appearance of your paragraphs. You can make bulleted lists and undo any mistakes you make while working with your document.

CHAPTER 4

Working With Pages

Introduction

So far, we've given you a basic page layout. It's the kind of document you would use for a letter, a resume, or a class essay. In this chapter, we're going to show you different ways to position the page and to put text on the page.

We're also going to use this chapter to show you how to use the ruler. It's an easy and visual way to set the margins for your text. You can also set different margins for different sections of text. For essay papers that are quoting long passages, the ability to set larger margins for quoted material will help make writing term papers a breeze.

Of course, with term papers, there are commands we'll get into later that will help you to cite your sources in the references sections of your term paper. But we're going to work up to that. For now, let's continue to build on the basic *Word* commands that we've learned so far.

The Ruler

Think of the ruler as one of those old fashioned wooden rulers laid down across the top of your page. The typical piece of paper that *Word* uses (and most printers have as a default setting) is 8-½ inches wide and 11 inches long.
When you open a new document, your ruler might not be displayed. It's a checkbox

that needs to be checked. To view the ruler, click on the View tab. Look at the *Show/Hide* group. Click on the box beside **Ruler** to add a checkmark.

 Put a checkmark in the **Ruler** checkbox in order to show the ruler when working on your document.

Now, when you look at your blank document, you should see a bar with numbers on it above the top of your document. These numbers represent inches, and they will help you to set margins in your text.

Figure 4-1 The Ruler

As you can see in the ruler in Figure 4-1, the "0" mark in the ruler does not start at the edge of the page. The "0" mark starts 1 inch from the edge of the page. That's because the left margin is set at 1 inch. The right edge of the page is at the 7-½ inches mark. When you add the left margin of 1 inch, you get the 8-½ inch standard width of the page.

There's also a ruler on the left side of the document window, a vertical ruler, but we're not going to concern ourselves with that one for now. Instead, let's focus on the horizontal ruler at the top of your document.

Why all the fuss about inches and margins and rulers?

Because they will help you to understand other commands and tools in *Word*

2007. We're going to cover **Tabs** next, and the ruler will provide you an excellent visual tool to lay out text in the way you want.

For now, let's look at how we can set margins and indents using the ruler.

Setting Margins and Indents with the Ruler

If you want to follow along, type three paragraphs into a new document in which you have the ruler turned on. We're going to write three paragraphs of a class term paper in which our second paragraph is going to be a long quotation. We'll quote a couple of authors, namely, us.

Because this term paper might be turned in to be graded, we'll need to follow MLA style for direct quotes of long passages. Long quotations will need to be indented one inch from the normal left margin.

It's easy with the ruler.

Here are our three paragraphs in our class assignment.

Figure 4-2 Our Term Paper

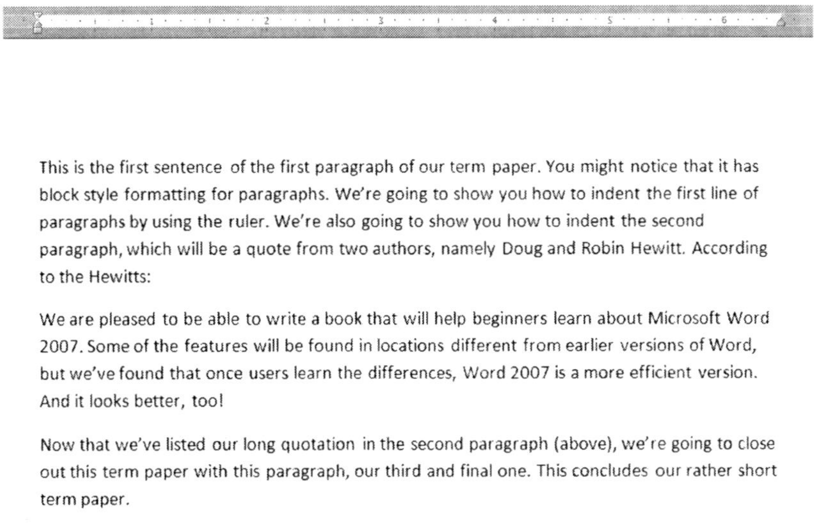

This is the first sentence of the first paragraph of our term paper. You might notice that it has block style formatting for paragraphs. We're going to show you how to indent the first line of paragraphs by using the ruler. We're also going to show you how to indent the second paragraph, which will be a quote from two authors, namely Doug and Robin Hewitt. According to the Hewitts:

We are pleased to be able to write a book that will help beginners learn about Microsoft Word 2007. Some of the features will be found in locations different from earlier versions of Word, but we've found that once users learn the differences, Word 2007 is a more efficient version. And it looks better, too!

Now that we've listed our long quotation in the second paragraph (above), we're going to close out this term paper with this paragraph, our third and final one. This concludes our rather short term paper.

Now, if you look at the left end of the ruler, you'll see a downward pointing arrowhead and an upward pointing arrowhead, and the arrowheads are pointing at each other. Under these arrowheads, there's a box. These are indicators that set the indents.

There are 3 indent controls at the left end of the ruler.

 Indent Controls. There is a down arrowhead, an up arrowhead, and a box at the bottom.

 Down Arrowhead. This sets the first line indent. Use this to indent the first line of a paragraph.

 Hanging Indent. The indent for the rest of paragraph.

 Both Indents. Moving the box will move both the first line indent and the hanging indent.

Let's set tasks using the three indent controls with the three paragraphs in our term paper.

Here's what we want to do.

- Change the first line indent for the first paragraphs to 0.5".
- Move the entire second paragraph indent in 1.0".
  This will make the second paragraph an accepted MLS style for a quoted paragraph. Note that if we had multiple paragraphs in a long quotation, all of which would be indented 1.0", the paragraphs within the long indented quotation would additionally have first lines indented an additional 0.5".
- Leave the first line of the third paragraph with no indent, but indent the rest of the paragraph 0.5".

In order to change these indents, select the paragraph, then move the ruler's indent controls as needed for that paragraph. Select the next paragraph, and move the ruler's indents for that paragraph. You'll see that the indents will affect only the selected paragraph.

Let's see what your paragraphs and rulers should look like for each paragraph.
First Paragraph

After you've changed the indent controls for the first paragraph, your document should look like the figure that follows. Note the position of the indent controls. The text in the figure is still highlighted, which means the indent controls for that paragraph will show in the ruler.

Figure 4-3 First Line Indent at 0.5″

This is the first sentence of the first paragraph of our term paper. You might notice that it has block style formatting for paragraphs. We're going to show you how to indent the first line of paragraphs by using the ruler. We're also going to show you how to indent the second paragraph, which will be a quote from two authors, namely Doug and Robin Hewitt. According to the Hewitts:

Second Paragraph
After you've selected the second paragraph and changed the hanging indent, you should see a ruler and document like the one in the figure that follows. Note the position of the arrowhead indent pointers!

Figure 4-4 Hanging and First Line Indent at 1.0"

This is the first sentence of the first paragraph of our term paper. You might notice that it has block style formatting for paragraphs. We're going to show you how to indent the first line of paragraphs by using the ruler. We're also going to show you how to indent the second paragraph, which will be a quote from two authors, namely Doug and Robin Hewitt. According to the Hewitts:

> We are pleased to be able to write a book that will help beginners learn about Microsoft Word 2007. Some of the features will be found in locations different from earlier versions of Word, but we've found that once users learn the differences, Word 2007 is a more efficient version. And it looks better, too!

Third Paragraph

After you've selected the third paragraph and changed both indents (by dragging the box), you should have a document that looks like the following figure. Note the indent control positions in the ruler!

Figure 4-5 Hanging Indent at 1.0"

> This is the first sentence of the first paragraph of our term paper. You might notice that it has block style formatting for paragraphs. We're going to show you how to indent the first line of paragraphs by using the ruler. We're also going to show you how to indent the second paragraph, which will be a quote from two authors, namely Doug and Robin Hewitt. According to the Hewitts:

> > We are pleased to be able to write a book that will help beginners learn about Microsoft Word 2007. Some of the features will be found in locations different from earlier versions of Word, but we've found that once users learn the differences, Word 2007 is a more efficient version. And it looks better, too!

> Now that we've listed our long quotation in the second paragraph (above), we're going to close out this term paper with this paragraph, our third and final one. This concludes our rather short term paper.

These exercises should give you a good feel for using the ruler and the indent controls. Note that you can select a paragraph and move the arrowhead at the right side of the ruler to change the left margin of your text.

Tabs

Look over to the left of the ruler, at the edge of the display. You'll see a small right angle in a box. This is the Tab control.

 Click on the button to select different type of tabs. When you click your pointer on the ruler, a tab will appear. The type of tab that appears is the one that is shown in this selection box.

A tab is a marker, a line in the sand, *per se*, and the words that you type as text will be aligned to the tab. Your text could be aligned to the left of the tab or to the right of the tab. There are other tab choices, too. Let's take a look.

Tab Selections

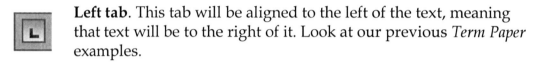

Left tab. This tab will be aligned to the left of the text, meaning that text will be to the right of it. Look at our previous *Term Paper* examples.

Center tab. The text you type after selecting this tab will be centered on the tab.

Right tab. This tab will be aligned to the right of the text, meaning that text will be to the left of it.

Decimal tab. Decreases the indent of the paragraph.

Bar Tab. This does not align text. It inserts a vertical bar at the position of the tab.

First Line Indent. This is not actually a tab, per se, but you can set the first line indent with this command. Another shortcut!

Hanging Indent. Again, not actually a tab. It's an alignment mark, though. Lines in a paragraph align to this mark.

Working With Tabs

So, how can the use of tabs help you work with *Word 2007*? The sky's the limit, but let's start with the realization that tabs are alignment tools. When you want aligned text, tabs are your tools.

Let's say that you want to start a birthday list. You might add to this list throughout the year as ideas occur to you. Making your list is easy with tabs.

John and Jill Q. Public have three children, whose names are Jeremy, Jill (named after her mother), and Jason.

They could make their list like this:

> *Jeremy: golf clubs, gift card ...*
> *Jill: purse, free spa visit ...*
> *Jason: bouncy ball, alphabet blocks ...*

But here's how to set up an easy tab list.

1. Open a new document.
2. Type "Family Birthday List"
3. Type "Jeremy", "Jill", and "Jason". Separate each name with a space.

Here's what your document should look like.

Figure 4-6 Family Birthday List (before tabs)

Family Birthday List

Jeremy Jill Jason

4. Next, select the first line (Family Birthday List) and click on the **Center** command in the *Paragraph* group.
5. Select the second line (Jeremy Jill Jason). With the text in the second line highlighted, click on the **Tab Control** until the *Center Tab* icon is shown.
6. Click on the ruler three times, at the 2" mark, the 3.5" mark, and the 5" mark.

Here's what your document should look like.

Figure 4-7 Setting Three Center Tabs (second line only)

Let's take a close-up look at the center tabs so you can see the alignment with the ruler markings.

Figure 4-8 Ruler With Three Center Tabs

Now, we need to align our three names (Jeremy, Jill, and Jason) with the tab settings.

7. Click your I-beam cursor in front of the J in Jeremy. Press **tab**.
8. Click your I-beam cursor in front of the J in Jill. Press **tab**.
9. Click your I-beam cursor in front of the J in Jason. Press **tab**.

It looks great, but we like for our "column" headers, the names of the birthday gift recipients, to stand apart, so let's underline them.

10. Select the line with Jeremy, Jill, and Jason in it.
11. Click on the **Underline** command in the Paragraph group.
12. Here's what your document should look like.

Figure 4-9 Underlined Birthday List

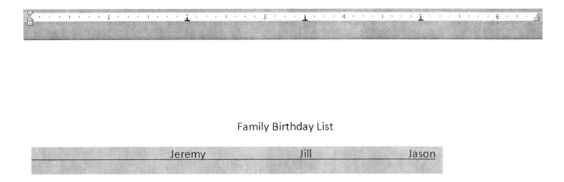

As you can see, the entire highlighted paragraph, or line of text, is underlined. This isn't what we wanted. We want only the words, which in this case are the names of our birthday gift recipients, underlined. So how do we change our Underline command to underline words only?

Easy!

13. Click on the **Font** command in the lower right corner of the *Font* group to show the *Font* dialog box.
14. Click on the down arrow in the **Underline Style:** command to open a menu of choices.

Figure 4-10 Underline Style

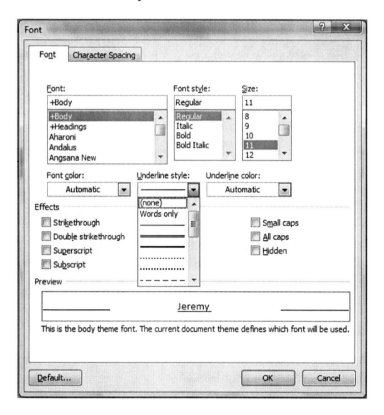

15. Select **Words only** and click OK.
16. Click elsewhere to deselect the text.
Here's what your document should look like.

Figure 4-11 Underlined Words Only

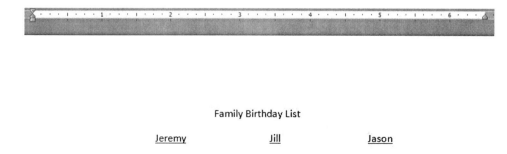

Family Birthday List

Jeremy   Jill   Jason

Okay, now that you have your tabs set up, we're going to go to the next line below the line with the names of Jeremy, Jill, and Jason. If your insertion point (cursor) is at the end of the word Jason and you press **enter**, you'll go to the next line, but you'll still have underlining turned on.

 When the insertion point (typically, your I-beam cursor) is at the end of a paragraph and you press **enter**, the formatting of that paragraph will be carried over to the next paragraph.

If your underlining is turned on, turn it off by toggling the command. Do this by selecting the current line of text (the birthday gifts line) and selecting the **Underline** command in the *Paragraph* group.

Now, we're ready to enter the presents for the birthday list.

17. Press **tab** and type "golf clubs."
18. Press **tab** and type "purse."
19. Press **tab** and type "bouncy ball."
20. Press **enter**.
21. Press **tab** and type "gift card."
22. Press **tab** and type "free spa visit."
23. Press **tab** and type "alphabet blocks."
24. Press **enter**.

Make your title of "Family Birthday List" bold by selecting the line and selecting **Bold** from the *Font* group.

Here's what your document should look like.

Figure 4-12 Family Birthday List

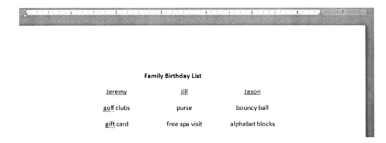

As you can see, you now have a birthday list that is visually appealing. You might notice the squiggly lines under golf and gift. These would not print out. They are an indication that there could be a grammar problem (namely, they're not capitalized). Don't worry. We'll cover how to turn this grammar-checking feature off later.

You can use the tab technique for other lists, including class essays and term papers.

Remember, tabs are a great way to align text. You can use tabs, too, for other purposes. The type of tab selected can provide great visual tools to help you make your documents appealing.

Tab Leaders

Tab leaders are a way to automatically insert characters in front of a tab. Let's add periods (or decimal points) between the gift items in our list of birthday presents.

With your Family Birthday List document open, select the Paragraph command in the Paragraph group. In the lower left corner of the dialog box, select the Tab command. Another dialog box opens.

You should see the Tab dialog box with the three tab settings. If not, go back and make sure your insertion point is in the area of your document that has those tab settings. Your title will not show the tab settings.

Figure 4-13 Tab Dialog Box

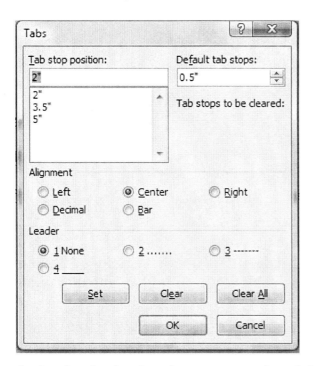

To set decimal point leaders for our second and third tab, select to highlight the two lines of gifts. Then:

1. Select "3.5"" in the tab box.
2. Select the circle beside the row of dots to select it in the *Leader* section.
3. Click on **OK**.
4. Repeat Steps 1 – 3 for the "5.0"" tab.

Here is how our list looks now.

Figure 4-14 Decimal Point Tab Leaders

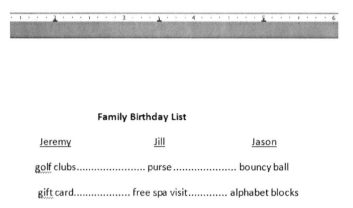

You can explore some of the other tab features, such as selecting a different leader, at your convenience. For now, let's move on to changing the layout of the page.

Page Layout

While much of our work uses the standard 8.5" by 11" page layout, there are times when we want the paper to be wider. By selecting a horizontal landscape for a page layout, we can have the effect of rotating the paper 90 degrees. One reason we might want to do this is to make a yard sale sign.
Follow these steps to create your yard sale sign.

1. Open *Word 2007*.
2. Select the **Page Layout** tab.
3. Select *Orientation*.
4. Select **Landscape**.

Figure 4-15 Landscape Page Layout

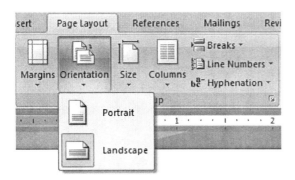

Note the width of the ruler above the document. The page is now 11″ wide.

Now that we have the page laid out in a landscape format, let's type our yard sale text. Make your own text or type along with us.

5. Type "Yard Sale".
6. Press enter.
7. Type "Saturday at 9:00 AM".
8. Select the first line of text and select a font size of **72**. (You might have to select the *Home* tab to access the *Font* group.)
9. Select the second line of text and select a font size of **48**.
10. Select both lines of text and select **Center** in the *Paragraph* group.

This works for all kinds of signs. You might, for example, want a DO NOT ENTER sign or DO NOT DISTURB. Here is what our sign looks like.

Figure 4-16 Yard Sale Sign

Use your creativity to come up with useful signs. We'll have ways to make your signs even more appealing later. For now, you can consider changing the color of your text in order to make it stand out more.

Conclusion

In this chapter, we showed you how to change the layout of your page. This is a great way to design your own signs.

We also covered tabs, how to set them and the different kinds of tabs. Tabs are often useful in making lists. While we were talking about tabs, we discussed the ruler and how to set tabs there. The ruler was also a useful tool to set margins and indents.

While we were doing this, we wrote *Our Term Paper* and our *Family Birthday List*. And, of course, we ended up with a *Yard Sale* sign.

CHAPTER 5

Spell Checking and Grammar Checking

Introduction

Now that you have some words on the page, let's look at some of the tools of *Word 2007* that you can use to make sure you're using the right words. In this chapter, we'll show you how to check the spelling in your document and the grammar of your text. We'll also look at some of the automatic formatting features. Last but not least, we'll delve into the automatic correction feature, which corrects text as you type. You might not even be aware of some of the changes that the automatic correction feature performs!

This is a beginner's book to *Microsoft Word 2007*, and there are some how-to books that will explain spell checking far in the advanced chapters. That's a shame, because it is a feature that is very basic, although it requires some degree of explanation in order to use it properly. And the same goes for grammar checking. Still, if you're looking to produce a document that has no spelling errors and is grammatically correct, the features in this chapter are essential. So, let's get to work!

Automated

Spell checking can be performed in two ways. You can wait until your document is finished and then select the Spelling & Grammar command to check the document, or you can have *Word* automatically check for spelling and grammar as you type. When a spelling error occurs, a red squiggly line will appear under the misspelled word. For grammar checking, a green squiggly line will appear beneath the word or words in question.

For some people, having their typing interrupted by squiggly lines can be distracting. They prefer to write full steam ahead and check for spelling and grammar later. Others like to correct errors as they go. Maybe they worry that they'll forget to check the spelling, which has certainly happened in many office settings.

To turn automated spelling and grammar checking on or off:
1. Open a new document.
2. Click on the **Microsoft Office** button.
3. Select the **Word Options** button near the bottom of the pane.
4. A dialog pane opens. Select **Proofing** in the left menu column.
5. The *Proofing* dialog box opens.

Figure 5-1 The Proofing Dialog Box

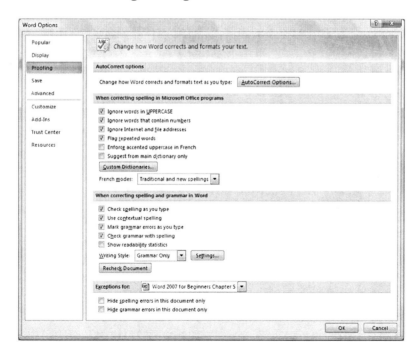

Spell Checking and Grammar Checking

There are a number of options we can select from the menu. For now, let's look at the automatic spelling and grammar checkboxes. These are the options that appear under the header bar titled *When correcting spelling and grammar in Word*.

These checkbox options can be seen in the following figure.

Figure 5-2 Automatic Spelling and Grammar Checkboxes

When correcting spelling and grammar in Word

- ☑ Check spelling as you type
- ☑ Use contextual spelling
- ☑ Mark grammar errors as you type
- ☑ Check grammar with spelling
- ☐ Show readability statistics

Writing Style: Grammar Only ▼ [Settings...]

[Recheck Document]

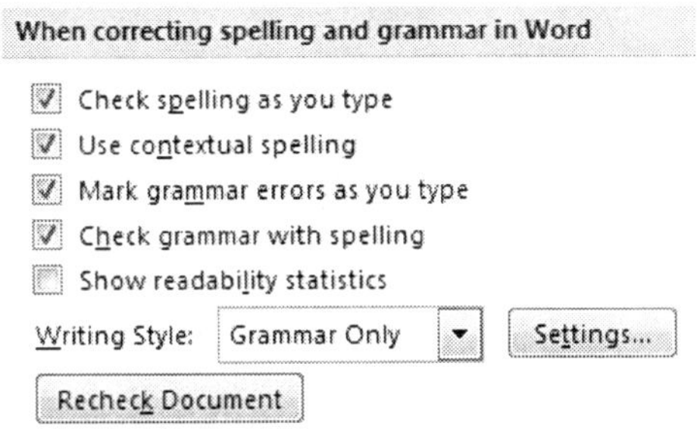

If you don't want the spelling and grammar checking to happen while you're typing, simply uncheck the boxes for *Check spelling as you type* and *Mark grammar errors as you type*.

Contextual spelling can help you to catch words that are spelled correctly for one meaning of the word, but it might not be the meaning you want to use. This can be helpful for people who aren't sure about the spellings of certain words.

Here's an example of when contextual spelling can catch a mistake. Contextual spelling errors appear as a squiggly blue line below the word in question.

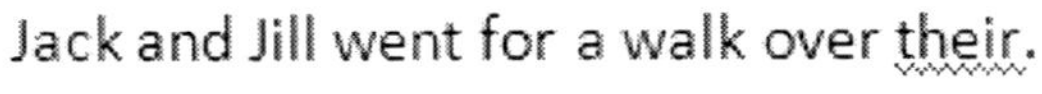

Jack and Jill went for a walk over their.

The word *their* is spelled correctly, but not in this context. The spelling should be *there*.

It should be noted that *Word* doesn't always get it right. That's why their suggested corrections are always *suggestions*. Use common sense when looking at suggested corrections. If you're not sure, ask for help or try finding your answer on the Internet.

There are many Internet sites with help for working with Word. Use a search engine and type in your question. Also, the Microsoft website has excellent help features. Search for "Microsoft Word Help" and you'll find it.

If you turn off automatic spelling and grammar checking, you can still check them after you're finishing writing. Simply click on the *Review* tab. You'll see the *Proofing* group at the left end of the *Ribbon*.

Click on the **Spelling & Grammar** button in the *Proofing* group under the *Review* tab to spell check and grammar check your document.

If you click on the **Spelling & Grammar** button, *Word* will progress through your document and ask you about each potential spelling or grammar error. In our example, *Word* notes that there could be a possible word choice error and highlights the word *their* in blue.

Figure 5-3 Spelling Suggestion

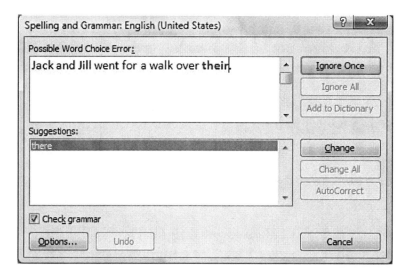

The *Spelling and Grammar* dialog box suggests a spelling of *there* in the *Suggestions*

box. If you want to take the suggestion, select the **Change** button. You can also select the **Ignore Once** button to ignore this single occurrence of the error. If the word or phrase in error occurs in multiple locations in the document, you'll also have the choice to select the **Ignore All** (occurrences) button.

You can also reach the *Word Options* dialog box by selecting the **Options** button in the lower left corner of the *Spelling and Grammar* dialog box. That's where you can select the *Proofing* pane and choose the checkboxes for automatic spelling and grammar checking (see Figure 5-1).

Automated Options

If you're typing text with the automatic spell and grammar checker turned on, the squiggly lines will appear in your document as you type them. But how do you access the dialog box with the suggested change?

Easy, just right click on the word in question.

Let's run through an example. We're going to purposefully misspell words and make a grammar error in the following sentence:
> *The rain in Spain stays mainly on the plain.*

Only we're going to type it like this:
> *The rain in Spain stay mainly on the plane.*

The words *rain in Spain stay* earns a squiggly line. When we right click anywhere in the words above the squiggly line, we get the following pop-up dialog boxes. Note that our mini-toolbar appears also.

Figure 5-4 Grammar Suggestion

You can see at the top of the grammar box that *Word* is suggesting two changes because the noun (*rain*) does not agree with the verb (*stay*). Either the *rains* have to stay or the *rain stays*. For our purpose, we would choose the first suggestion. Choose the first line by clicking on it, and *Word* makes the correction in our document.

There are some other options with the pop-up grammar box.

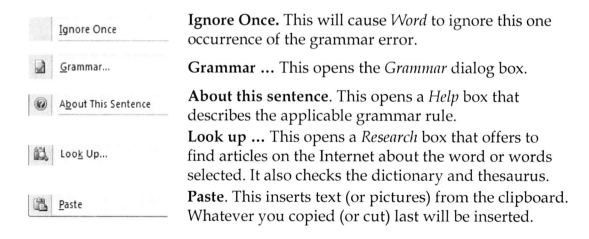

Ignore Once. This will cause *Word* to ignore this one occurrence of the grammar error.

Grammar … This opens the *Grammar* dialog box.

About this sentence. This opens a *Help* box that describes the applicable grammar rule.

Look up … This opens a *Research* box that offers to find articles on the Internet about the word or words selected. It also checks the dictionary and thesaurus.

Paste. This inserts text (or pictures) from the clipboard. Whatever you copied (or cut) last will be inserted.

The *Grammar* dialog box offers a few additional options for the *Word* user. If you click on **Grammar ...**, you'll see another pop-up window.

 If at any point while reading this book, you would like to learn more about a topic, click on the question mark in the upper right corner of the screen, just above the *Ribbon*. You can explore topics when they interest you, which will help you to learn them.

Figure 5-5 Grammar Dialog Box

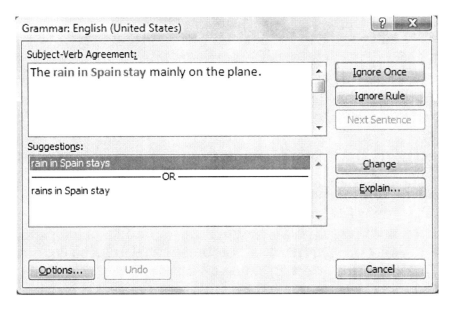

Here are your options for commands in the Grammar dialog box.

- **Ignore Once.** *Word* will ignore this one occurrence of the broken grammar rule.
- **Ignore Rule.** *Word* will ignore all occurrences of this rule being broken in the document.
- **Change.** Will change the underlined text to the text highlighted in the *Suggestions* box.
- **Explain.** *Word* opens a *Help* box that attempts to explain the grammar rule.
- **Options.** Opens the *Proofing* pane in the *Word Options* box.

You might also notice that the word *plane* did not earn a squiggly line. As anyone who might have heard this expression before knows, the rain in Spain is on the *plain*, not the *plane*. That's one more reason to read over your documents after finishing them, even if you've done spell checking with *Word*. We'll leave it to you to purposefully misspell a word and see how you can have *Word* correct it. Simply right click on the misspelled word and select the correct spelling in the dialog box.

Autocorrect

Word 2007 corrects some mistakes automatically as you type. For example, some people might have the **shift** button depressed too long when capitalizing the first word in a sentence. This would cause the second letter in the word to also be capitalized. *Word* recognizes this as a common error and automatically corrects it by changing the second letter to lower case.

To open the *Autocorrect* dialog box:

1. Open a new document.
2. Click on the **Microsoft Office** button.
3. Select the **Word Options** button near the bottom of the pane.
4. A dialog pane opens. Select **Proofing** in the left menu column.
5. Click on **AutoCorrect Options ...** button
6. The *AutoCorrect* dialog box opens.

Figure 5-6 AutoCorrect Dialog Box

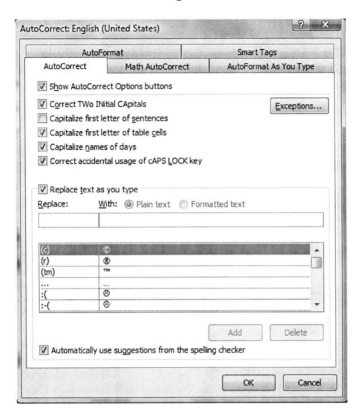

You can see five different tabs in the *AutoCorrect* dialog box. The *AutoCorrect* tab is the default tab. Here you can check boxes that direct *Word* to correct items as they are typed. We've already talked about the first two letters of a word being capitalized, a correction rule identified in the second checkbox.

But what if you were writing about identification cards and wanted to shorten it to IDs? The first two letters in IDs are capitalized. This is called an exception. If you click on the **Exceptions** button, you'll see *ID* is an exception to the rule. You can enter other exceptions to the rule from here.

As you can see in the *AutoCorrect* dialog box, *Word* will capitalize days of the week automatically if you forget. It also corrects for accidentally setting the **caps lock** key.

Word will also capitalize the first words in the cells of a table. We'll talk about tables later.

At the bottom, you can see that *Word* will insert frown faces when you type a certain sequence of letters and characters. Use the scroll bar to see what other icons and symbols *Word* will automatically change when it sees those specific combinations.

We're not going to worry about the *Math AutoCorrect* and the *SmartTags* tabs in this book, but you can type those subjects into *Word Help* if you want to read about them.

For now, let's move on to the *AutoFormat* tabs.

AutoFormat

Click on the *AutoFormat* tab to take a look at the *AutoFormat* dialog box.

Figure 5-7 AutoFormat Dialog Box

As you can see, some of these formatting commands cover areas that this book hasn't yet delved into. That's ok. We'll talk about styles and bulleted lists later.

For now, let's look at the four most important features on this pane and what they do.

- **"Straight quotes" with "smart quotes"** Straight quotes are used for denoting inches. Note that if you want straight quotes, simply click on **Undo** after *Word* performs the automatic formatting function.
- **Ordinals (1st) with superscript** When you type 1st, *Word* will replace it with 1st.
- **Fractions (1/2) with fraction character (½)** When you type 1/2, *Word* will replace it with ½.
- **Hyphens (--) with dash (—)** Type two dashes in a row and *Word* will replace it with a dash.

Now let's look at the *AutoFormat As You Type* tab.

AutoFormat As You Type

Click on the AutoFormat tab to take a look at the AutoFormat dialog box.

Figure 5-8 AutoFormat As You Type Dialog Box

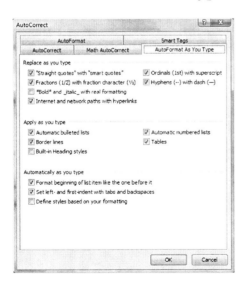

We've already talked about many of these checkbox rules. The difference here is that these automatic formatting changes will occur as you type.

If you have *AutoFormat as you type* turned off, you can still automatically format a document. To do that, we're going to add the **AutoFormat Now** command to the *Quick Access Toolbar*, which is the toolbar beside the **Microsoft Office** button.

Adding Command to Quick Access Toolbar

These are the steps to add the **AutoFormat Now** command to the *Quick Access Toolbar*. When you have time, look through the other commands that you can add. If you find a command that you use often, these are the steps to adding the command. They're the same steps to add any command.

1. Open a new document.
2. Click on the **Customize Quick Access Toolbar** button, which is the rightmost command on the *Quick Access Toolbar*.
3. Select **More Commands ...**
4. Select **All Commands** from the *Choose commands from* drop-down menu.
5. A list of commands appears for you to select from. Scroll down by using the side scroll bar to find **AutoFormat Now**.

Figure 5-9 Customize Quick Access Toolbar

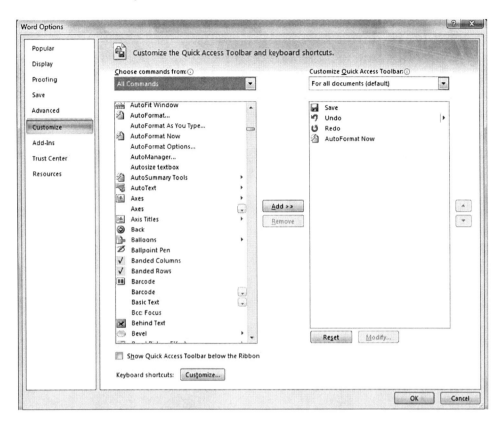

6. Select **AutoFormat Now**.
7. Click on the **Add >>** command button.
8. Click **OK**.

You now have the **AutoFormat Now** command on your *Quick Access Toolbar*. If you have automatic formatting turned off, click on the **AutoFormat Now** command button in your *Quick Access Toolbar* to apply the formatting rules you've selected in this chapter.

Summary

In this chapter, we've shown how you can perform spell checking and grammar checking on your documents. You can do this as you type, or you can wait until you're finished with the document, then go back and perform the functions. You can also perform formatting features in the same way.

We've shown you a great way to customize your *Quick Access Toolbar*, making command buttons that you use frequently available no matter which tab you're working with and which commands are shown in the *Ribbon*.

By using the features in this chapter, you can go a long way in making your documents more professional, and you just might learn a little about grammar along the way.

CHAPTER 6

Headers and Footers

Introduction

You should feel comfortable now in knowing how to be reasonably sure your *Word* documents have words that are correctly spelled.

In this chapter, we're going to go over headers and footers. These two terms are aptly named. Just as the head is at the top of the body, the header is at the top of the page. And of course the foot and footer are at the bottom of the body and page respectively.

If you have ever read a novel, you'll notice that the title of the book (sometimes) and the page number are at the top or bottom of each page. These are headers or footers. Sometimes the author name is included.

Why bother with headers and footers at all?

Headers and footers help readers know where they're at in a document. The location can be identified by page number, section number, or chapter. Also, page numbering is automated, saving time. Imagine the old days when page numbers had to be inserted manually!

In a classroom chemistry report, you could have a header that breaks the report down into *Procedure* and *Results*, for example. And if it's a printed report and the pages are dropped, having numbered pages can help put it back together with the pages in order.

Insert a Header

Let's open a new document and place a header in it. We're going to write a report about a book we have read. It's an imaginary book we're calling *The Romans Spoke Latin But It's All Greek to Me*.

To give a document a header:

1) Open a new document.
2) Position the pointer at the top of the page.
3) Double click.
4) The *Header & Footer Design Ribbon* opens.

Notice that the *Ribbon* is populated by new *Groups*. Also, a new *Tab* has appeared. The new *Tab* is titled *Design*. The groups in this *Ribbon* are associated with the *Header & Footer Design* tab.

Figure 6-1 The Header & Footer Design Ribbon

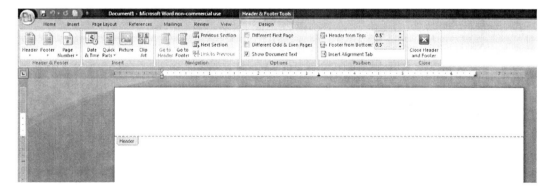

Now, let's put the title of our book report into the header. Type the name. You might have to click your pointer in the header area (above the dashed line) to move your insertion point to the header, but it should be there when you open the *Header & Footer Ribbon*.

Figure 6-2 Document Title as Header Text

Notice that we have italicized our title. You can select the text, and then go to the *Home* tab and select **Italics** or de-select it depending on your preferences. You could also select the text and pick **Italics** from the mini-Toolbar.

Also notice that the ruler is shown. You can position the text in the *Header* in the same way that text in the document is positioned via *Ruler* settings.

Positioning and Page Numbering

We want our header to be centered on each page of our report.

1) Select the text in the header.
2) Go to the *Home* tab.
3) Select **Center** in the *Paragraph* group.

Figure 6-3 Centered Header Text

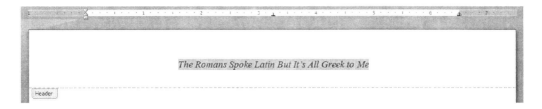

Note that the text is still highlighted. You have to click your pointer somewhere in the active writing area (in this case, somewhere in the *Header*) to de-select the text.

 Microsoft Word 2007 is like other *Word* applications. When text is selected and an operation is performed on the selected text, the text will stay selected until you de-select the text.

Now let's add a page number. Some people prefer simply to have the page number on the header. Other people like to type "page" then add a space and the number. Still other people like to type "p." and then have the number. Choose whichever appeals to you most.

4) To add the page number:
5) Click at the end of the header text.
6) Tap the spacebar twice.
7) Type "page".
8) Tap the spacebar once.
9) Select the *Insert* tab. (Optional.)
10) Find the *Header & Footer* group. Note: this group also appears on the *Design* tab.

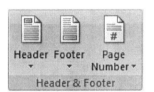 This is the *Header & Footer* group. Note that **Page Number** has an arrowhead to open a list of commands.

11) Click on **Page Number** in the *Header & Footer* group.
You'll see that you have some choices of commands.

Figure 6-4 Page Number Commands

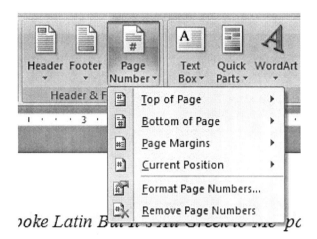

We've already positioned our cursor where we want to put the page number, so let's select the current position.

12) Select **Current Position**.

You'll see that *Word* gives you more choices.

Figure 6-5 Current Position Commands

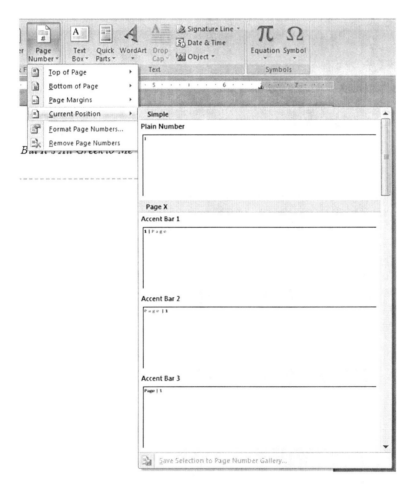

We're not going to worry about the *Accent Bars*. If you want to play with those, select them. For now, we're going with a beginner's choice.

13) Select **Plain Number**.
14) Select the *Design* tab if you're currently under the *Insert* tab.
15) Click on **Close Header and Footer**.

Congratulations! You now have a page number and the title of your report at the top of your page. When you type your report, the header will appear at the top of each page. The page number will increment and show the actual number of the page.

Page Numbers

You don't have to type text into a header when you just want the page number. Simply go to the *Insert* tab and find the *Header & Footer* group. Select **Page Number**, then select the position for your page number. Some of the options will have "Page" already in it, so *Word* does it for you.

Different First Page

You may have noticed a command called **Format Page Number ...** when you clicked on the **Page Number** command to open a list of numbering commands.

 Format Page Numbers...

This is the **Format Page Numbers ...** command.

Go back to your book report and open the header. Click on **Page Number** and then click on **Format Page Numbers ...**. You'll see another set of commands.

Figure 6-6 Page Number Format

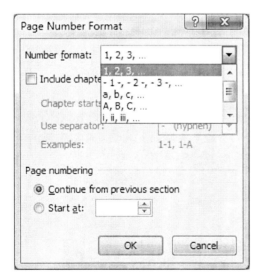

In this box, you can select the kind of numbering you want. You could "number" your pages with successive letters or Roman numerals. You can also click on the **Start at:** option and start you page numbering at a number other than 1. This is useful if you're working on several sections of a report, and each section has its own *Word* file. You can start numbering the second section with the page number after the last page number of the first section.

Footers

We're going to make this simple. The only difference between the *Footer* commands and the *Header* commands is the position on the page. Everything we're showing you in the *Header* also applies to the *Footer*. If you want your report title and page numbers at the bottom of the page, you simple repeat the steps except double clicking at the bottom of the page to open the *Header & Footer Design* tab and begin editing in the footer area (bottom) of the page.

Note that you can also access the *Header & Footer Design Ribbon* from the *Insert* tab and selecting the **Header** or **Footer** command. Try each method and see which one feels more comfortable for you.

Also note that if you already have a header or footer in your document, this is where you select the command to edit them.

Header & Footer Design

The *Header & Footer Design* tab, as we've pointed out, opens a new *Ribbon* with new groups. Let's take a look at these groups and see what the commands do. Here's a closer look at the *Header & Footer Design* ribbon.

Figure 6-7 Header & Footer Design Ribbon

The first group is the *Header & Footer* group.

Header & Footer Group

Part of the reason we're writing this book is to help beginner's become familiar with *Word* commands, with the *Word* interface on the computer monitor, and to help you become more comfortable and confident that you can accomplish whatever you want with the appearance of your document. To that end, we might have repeat pictures of groups in several places in this book. That's okay. We want you to become more familiar with the appearance of these groups.

Figure 6-8 Header & Footer Group

We've already talked about these commands, but we'll summarize them here.

 Header This command allows you to select from several *header* templates. It also has the **Remove Header** and **Edit Header** commands.

 Footer This command allows you to select from several *footer* templates. It also has the **Remove Footer** and **Edit Footer** commands.

 Page Number This command gives you options of where to insert the page number. It also has the **Format Page Numbers ...** and **Remove Page Numbers** commands.

Insert Group

This group allows you to insert various items into the header.

Figure 6-9 Insert Group

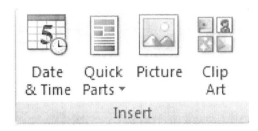

Here's a breakdown of each command.

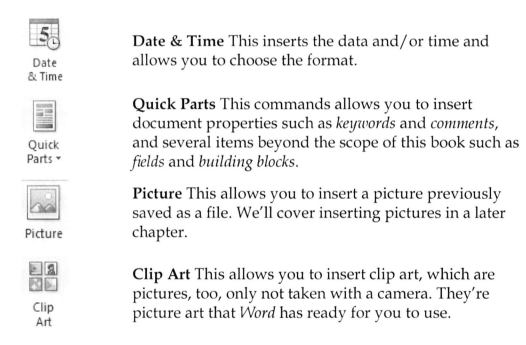

Date & Time This inserts the data and/or time and allows you to choose the format.

Quick Parts This commands allows you to insert document properties such as *keywords* and *comments*, and several items beyond the scope of this book such as *fields* and *building blocks*.

Picture This allows you to insert a picture previously saved as a file. We'll cover inserting pictures in a later chapter.

Clip Art This allows you to insert clip art, which are pictures, too, only not taken with a camera. They're picture art that *Word* has ready for you to use.

Navigation Group

Want to move around from header to footer, from one page to the next while editing headers and footers? The *Navigation* group is the place to be!

Figure 6-10 Navigation Group

Here's a summary of the commands in the *Navigation* group.

Go to Header This switches you to the header to edit it if you're editing the footer. The command is grayed out if you're already working in the header.

Go to Footer This switches you from editing the header to the footer.

Section Commands When you insert section breaks, you can move to headers (and footers) associated with a previous or with the next section. This is useful if you're writing a novel and you want the chapter number in the header. Simply create section breaks and different headers for the specific sections.

Options Group

The *Options* group gives you some choices for setting up your headers and footers.

Figure 6-11 Options Group

Let's look at each of these optional commands in the *Options* group.

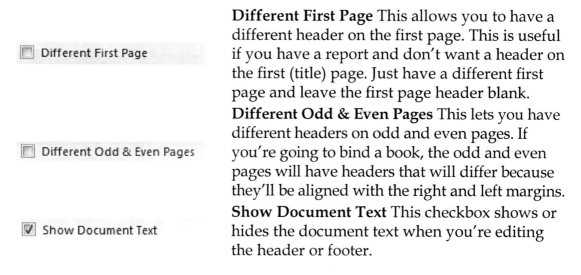

Different First Page This allows you to have a different header on the first page. This is useful if you have a report and don't want a header on the first (title) page. Just have a different first page and leave the first page header blank.

Different Odd & Even Pages This lets you have different headers on odd and even pages. If you're going to bind a book, the odd and even pages will have headers that will differ because they'll be aligned with the right and left margins.

Show Document Text This checkbox shows or hides the document text when you're editing the header or footer.

Position Group

Commands in the *Position* group place your headers and footers where you want them.

Figure 6-12 Position Group

With the commands in this group, you can position you headers and footers, say, a half inch from the edge of the page. That's the default distance, but you can change it if you want.

 Some printers cannot print closer than a set distance from the edge of the paper. If you're printing documents, make sure your headers and footers will print. If not, move them farther from the edge of the paper.

Let's take a look at the commands in the *Position* group.

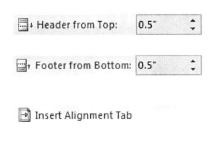 **Header from Top:** This allows you to set the distance for the header text from the top of the page.

Footer from Bottom: This allows you to set the distance for the footer text from the bottom of the page.

Insert Alignment Tab This allows you to inset a tab in the header. This tab applies only to the header (or footer) and not the document text.

Close Group

There's only one command in this group, so it's hardly worth calling a group, but that's the way the *Headers & Footers Design* ribbon comes to us, and we're just the messengers here.

Figure 6-13 Close Group

This command closes the *Headers & Footers Design* ribbon. The headers and footers editing areas will close. That is, they will become grayed out so that they can no longer be edited, until, that is, you open the *Headers & Footers Design*

ribbon again.

 If you make a mistake, click on **Undo**. It works just the same when you're editing headers and footers.

Summary

In this chapter, we've shown you how to work with headers and footers. This could be a class formatting requirement for your term papers. Many teachers want your name on each page, especially if it's a printed report.

We've also shown how you can insert page numbering into your document. The page numbering can be in a variety of formats and located in different areas of each page.

Reports and class assignments typically have a first page that could be considered a title page. The title page might have the student's name and class name. It might have the semester and year listed. You wouldn't want the header to show that it's page 1 because it's obviously the first page. So we've shown you how to locate the **Different First Page** checkbox.

We've shown you the commands in the *Headers & Footers Design* ribbon. If headers and footers are important to you, take the time to explore the different commands and how they affect the appearance of your headers and footers.

CHAPTER 7

Inserting Pictures

Introduction

The *Insert* tab brings with it a powerful ribbon. With it, you can insert all sorts of wonderful things into your document. We're going to cover some of these options in later chapters. For example, we'll devote an entire chapter to tables, which can be inserted with the **Table** command under the *Insert* tab.

For now, we want to keep our outlook that this is a book for beginners, and we're going to cover the *Illustrations* group under the *Insert* tab. To start with, we'll show you how to insert pictures.

These pictures can be in the form of a file that you saved from your camera, or they can be clipart, which are drawings and pictures that come with *Word*. We will also be showing how to insert a text box. Text boxes are great ways to associate text with a picture. You can insert other things, too, like arrows. Then you can arrange the arrows to point at objects in your picture, such as a test tube in a chemistry lab or a spot on the beach where you went swimming last year. We'll also show you a few formatting commands to help you get a fast start on making the most of your inserted pictures.

Insert a Picture

We're going to assume you know at this stage how to open a file, so we're going to start abbreviating some of our step-by-step instructions. But don't worry; we won't jump too far ahead.

In our instructions, we'll be asking you to type some text. This is so that you'll know how the text is affected by the picture you insert. The picture or clipart you're going to insert will be inserted at the insertion point. You'll be able to move the picture or clipart after insertion, but it's always helpful to know ahead of time where the picture will appear.

It might be helpful at this point for you to think about how you'll be using *Word*. If you're going to write family update letters, write a practice letter when a step says to type some text. If you're writing reports for school, type in an imaginary report. The more practice you get, the better you'll become with *Word*.

So let's get started.

1) Open a new document.
2) Type some text, say two or three paragraphs.
3) Click on the *Insert* tab.
4) Find the *Illustrations* group. We're going to cover the various commands in the *Illustrations* group later in this chapter. For now, we want you to see where we're working.

Figure 7-1 The Illustrations Group

5) Click on **Picture**.

The *Insert Picture* dialog box appears.

Figure 7-2 The Insert Picture Dialog Box

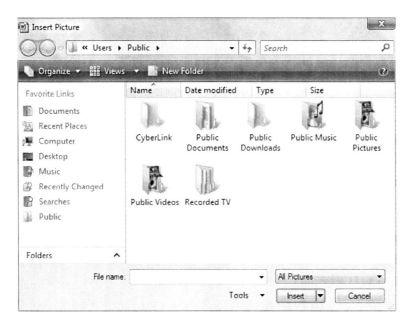

This is how to insert a picture from a file. Find your file from your *Desktop*, from your *Documents* folder, or from wherever you have them stored. If you have them on a flash drive, you can click on *Computer* and find your flash drive there.

For now, let's pretend we're going to change our mind, now that we have the *Insert Picture* dialog box open. We'll cancel out of this box and go to the **Clip Art** command.

6) Click on **Cancel** in the *Insert Picture* dialog box.
7) Select **Clip Art**.
8) The *Clip Art* pane opens.

Figure 7-3 The Clip Art Pane

We're not going to go into depth on explaining what you can do with the *Clip Art* pane, which appears on the right side of the *Word* display, but we want to point out a few options in this pane. First, here's what we're planning to do. We'll scroll down the list of pictures (clipart figures) and select one with our pointer. The picture will appear in our document at our insertion point. Our insertion point will be at the bottom of our text, as we don't want the picture interfering with our text layout. Besides, we haven't decided yet where to place the picture.

What other actions could you do from the Clip Art pane?

- **Search for:** Search your computer or selected folders for clip art with a specific file name.
- **Search in:** You can organize your clip art in separate collection locations.
- **Results should be:** You can select photographs, movies, sounds, and clipart.
- **Organize clips ...** Opens an organizer pane so you can see the file locations.
- **Clip art on Office Online** Go online and search the Microsoft

collection of clipart.
- **Tips for finding clips** A help button for help specific to clipart.
- **X button** It's in the upper right corner of the pane. You'll need to select **X** to exit the pane.

Now, let's get back to our assignment. Remember, we've typed our text into a new document, and now we're going to insert a picture.

9) Use the scroll bar to find the picture you want.
10) Click on the picture.
11) Click on the **X** to exit the *Clip Art* pane.

Here's how our assignment looks at this point.

Figure 7-4 Inserted Clipart

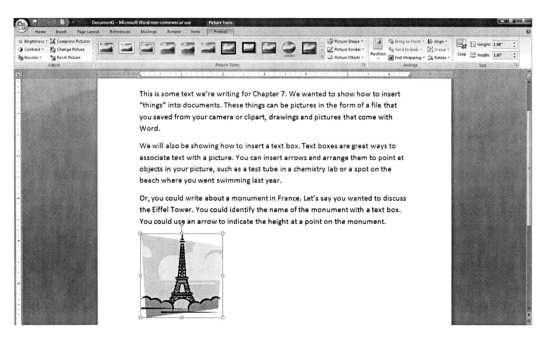

We want to point out a few things before moving on.
Note that this clipart picture is still selected.

Just like text that has been selected and moved (or has had some operation performed on it), the picture will stay selected until you deselect it by clicking your pointer somewhere else in the document.

Also note the small circles at the corners and sides of the picture. These are *handles*. If you move your pointer over a handle, press the left mouse button down, and drag your pointer while continuing to keep the button pressed down, you can manually change the size of your picture.

The small circle above the picture allows you to rotate the picture via the same, press-button-and-drag method.

Also, the ribbon has changed. Because you have inserted a picture, *Word* automatically switches the ribbon to the *Format Ribbon* for a new *Picture Tools* tab. We'll use a few of the commands in this *Format Ribbon* to reposition our picture. For now, let's just deselect the picture.

The Picture Tools Format Ribbon

When you deselect the picture, you might lose the *Picture Tools Format* ribbon, which is what we want to talk about. So how do you get the ribbon back? Click on the picture and select the *Picture Tools Format* tab.

Okay. Now that you have the ribbon back in view, let's take a look at it.

Figure 7-5 The Picture Tools Format Ribbon

In the middle part of the ribbon, you'll see some different frames and effects you can apply to your picture. These are in the *Picture Styles* group. We won't go over each one, but you could select a nice frame for your picture.

Let's take a moment to look at some of the other groups. We're going to position our picture manually, and we're going to set the size by dragging a handle, but if you wanted to do things differently you could use this ribbon to accomplish the same effects.

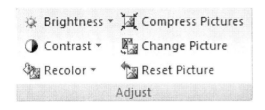

Brightness Changes brightness of picture.
Contrast Changes contrast of picture.
Recolor Change color modes (such as black and white) and alter picture shades.
Compress Pictures Reduces the file size of the picture (useful for large files).
Change Picture Swaps the selected picture with another one that you get to select
Reset Picture Removes changes you've made to the picture

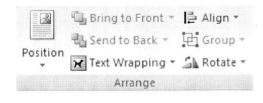

Picture Shape Select from a large list of shapes for your picture.
Picture Border Select colors and styles for the picture border.
Picture Effects Choose an effect such as a shadow or bevel for your picture.

Bring to Front A layering command.
Send to Back Another layering command.
Text Wrapping Select the way text appears when it is near your picture
Align Choose from a variety of alignment options for your picture such as centered.
Group Make several pictures combine into one object you can perform operations on.
Rotate Choose from different rotation commands, including upside down.

Crop Cut off sections of the picture. Select this command, then move the picture handles to cut.
Height, Width: Manually select the size of your picture.
Arrow Launcher Opens *Size* dialog box with additional commands.

Picture Commands

Like we indicated earlier, we're going to perform some commands on our picture and hopefully give you ideas on what to do with yours. First, we're going to move our picture up and have the text nestled up nicely right beside it. We do this with a feature called text wrapping.

1) Select your picture.
2) Select **Text Wrapping** in the *Arrange* group.
3) Select **Tight**. (Note your other options for your later personal use.)
4) Click on the picture.
5) With your pointer over the picture, depress the left mouse button.
6) Keep the mouse button depressed and drag your picture up.
7) Release the mouse button.

You should have a document that now has a picture with text wrapped around it. See how ours looks. You can drag the picture higher or lower per your preferences.

Figure 7-6 Text Wrapping Around Picture

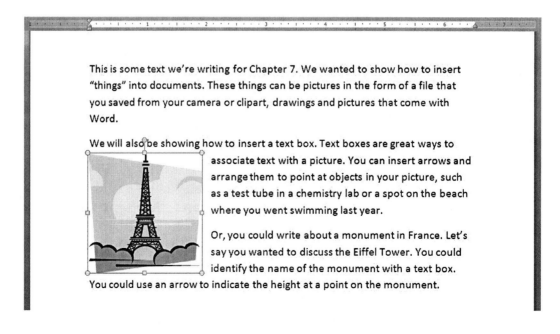

This is some text we're writing for Chapter 7. We wanted to show how to insert "things" into documents. These things can be pictures in the form of a file that you saved from your camera or clipart, drawings and pictures that come with Word.

We will also be showing how to insert a text box. Text boxes are great ways to associate text with a picture. You can insert arrows and arrange them to point at objects in your picture, such as a test tube in a chemistry lab or a spot on the beach where you went swimming last year.

Or, you could write about a monument in France. Let's say you wanted to discuss the Eiffel Tower. You could identify the name of the monument with a text box. You could use an arrow to indicate the height at a point on the monument.

What you want to keep in mind here is that you have other options for how the picture is aligned with the page and with the text. You can align it with the right side of the page, center it, make it bigger, put a frame around it, and change the coloring.

 Now is a good time to look at some of the other text wrapping options. Select the picture, then select the **Text Wrapping** command. Select another text wrapping option, such as **In Line with Text**. Look at how it affects your document. Click **Undo** to change back. Move the picture around within the text and see the results. This is a valuable strategy to learn how *Word* commands affect the appearance of your document.

All of the alignment commands are available for you on the *Picture Tools Format* ribbon. Just keep in mind that you will need to have your picture selected when you perform an operation on it.

You'll know the picture is selected because it will have the handles (small circles) surrounding it in the borders.

So now, let's add a text box to identify our picture.

Add Text Box

There are about a zillion things you can do with text boxes. Other books will go into great detail about those commands. We're going to sidestep most of them. Keep in mind that a text box is exactly what it sounds like, a box on the page that you can fill with text. But the neat thing about text boxes is, you can move them around and change the properties just like you can with pictures.

> To add a text box:
> 1) Click on the *Insert* tab.
> 2) Click on **Text Box** in the *Text* group.
> 3) Select **Simple Text Box**.

If you want to explore some additional options later, select a different style of text box. But for now, you should have a *Word* document with a text box inserted at where you last left your insertion point.

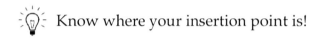 Know where your insertion point is!

Here is our document:

Figure 7-7 Insert Text Box

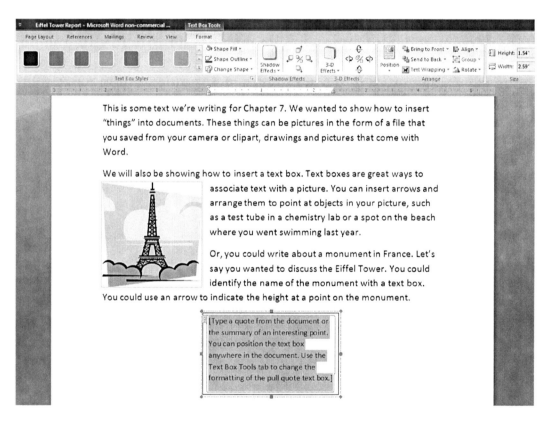

Note that the text in the text box is already highlighted. You could hit delete and start typing text, or you can simply start typing text (selected text is automatically deleted).

Also note that you have a new ribbon.

This ribbon is called the *Text Box Tools* ribbon. It has a lot of commands and groups that are similar to the *Picture Tools Format* ribbon, and we're not going to go into the groups. We're trying to make this book ideal for beginners, so understand that you don't *need* to know all of those commands. You've inserted a text box, so all you need to do now is type you text, re-size the text box, and move the text box where you want it. If you want to explore text box commands, open Help and type the text box command into the search box to learn more.

Working with a Text Box

We want to identify our picture as the Eiffel Tower, so with the text selected in your text box (or the text deleted), type "Eiffel Tower". Here's how our text box looks after we type that text.

Figure 7-8 Inserted Text in Text Box

 We will also be showing how to insert a text box. Text boxes are great ways to associate text with a picture. You can insert arrows and arrange them to point at objects in your picture, such as a test tube in a chemistry lab or a spot on the beach where you went swimming last year.

Or, you could write about a monument in France. Let's say you wanted to discuss the Eiffel Tower. You could identify the name of the monument with a text box.

You could use an arrow to indicate the height at a point on the monument.

Eiffel Tower

Note that there are two major problems with our text box.
- The box is much too big for our two simple words.
- The box does not identify the picture because they are not near each other.

In order to correct the size of the text box, remember that a text box is like a picture in that it has "handles." We're going to click on the center handle in the right border of the text box and drag it to the left. Then we'll click on the center handle in the bottom border of the text box and drag it slightly up.

We should now have a nicely sized text box for the text we've typed. You can re-size your text box to whatever size pleases you.

Figure 7-9 Re-sized Text Box

 Or, you could write about a monument in France. Let's say you wanted to discuss the Eiffel Tower. You could identify the name of the monument with a text box. You could use an arrow to indicate the height at a point on the monument.

Now, let's move the text box into the bottom of the picture. Then, visually, it will be an announcement of what the picture is, acting as a label. To move the text box, you have to select it.

 If the text box is too small, part of your text will be hidden. Your text still exists, but you can't see it. Select a text box handle and enlarge the box until all of your text is visible.

There's a common problem with trying to move a text box. You could try to select it by clicking on it, and you could have entered into the text editing mode. This is the mode in which you're typing text into the box. If you click and drag while in this mode, you're going to simply select text in the text box. This is the same way to select any other kind of text in your document. You depress the left mouse key, drag the mouse, and text becomes highlighted until you lift up on the left mouse key.

In order to select the text box as an object (a moveable object), you sometimes will have to click elsewhere in the document first, then re-select the text box by clicking your pointer on the border of it. If you click in the middle area, Word thinks you want to work with the text instead of the box.

Usually, it's easiest to click in the space just above the text box, then lower the pointer to the top border, then left click.

Now that the text box is selected, put your pointer on the top border, left click, and move your mouse. Your text box will move with your mouse movements. Position the text box over the bottom of the picture and release the mouse button. Here's how our document looks.

Figure 7-10 Text Box Over Picture

We will also be showing how to insert a text box. Text boxes are great ways to associate text with a picture. You can insert arrows and arrange them to point at objects in your picture, such as a test tube in a chemistry lab or a spot on the beach where you went swimming last year.

Or, you could write about a monument in France. Let's say you wanted to discuss the Eiffel Tower. You could identify the name of the monument with a text box. You could use an arrow to indicate the height at a point on the monument.

Insert Arrow

Let's have our report be informative. How tall is the top of the Eiffel Tower? We can show the reader by pointing at the top of the tower with an arrow and adding another text box with the height listed.

We're hoping in this chapter to steer you toward opportunities on how to present your information in a visual way. As much as we enjoy writing, a well-positioned picture and arrow can speak volumes, and visual information is often retained better than the written word.

So:

1) Position your insertion point at the bottom of your document.
2) Select the *Insert* tab.
3) Click on **Shapes**.
4) Select the **Line** with a single arrowhead.

You can, of course, select any shape you want. It's easy to get overwhelmed, though. We have found that often the simple choice is the best choice. So what not select a simple arrow to point at what you want to highlight?

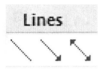

These represent just a few of the selections you can insert from the *Insert* tab, in the *Illustrations* group, with the **Shapes** command. We like the line with a single arrowhead so we can point at what the text is referring to.

To insert the arrow, we're going to click once to start the arrow, then click again to end the arrow.

5) Move your pointer over an area of the document with no text.
6) Click once.
7) Drag your cursor to the right an inch or two.
8) Click again.

Here's what your screen should show after you select a line with an arrowhead.

Figure 7-11 Inserted Arrow

We will also be showing how to insert a text box. Text b
associate text with a picture.
arrange them to point at obje
as a test tube in a chemistry I
where you went swimming la

Or, you could write about a m
say you wanted to discuss the
identify the name of the mon

You could use an arrow to indicate the height at a point

Modifying an AutoShape

Note that the arrow has a small circle at each end. These are the handles, just like a picture has handles. With an arrow, though, we can do a few special tricks. Let's say we want to point the arrow at the top of the Eiffel Tower (not the antenna, though).

First we'll want the arrow to stand out more. Let's make it thicker.
1) Select the arrow by clicking on it.
2) Right click.
3) The *Format AutoShape* dialog box appears.

Figure 7-12 Format AutoShape Dialog Box

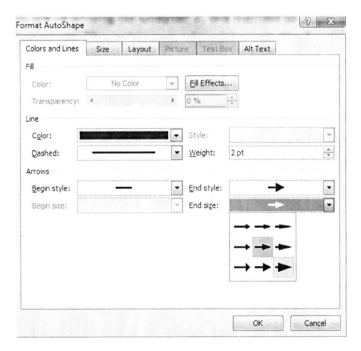

You'll notice you can change the style of the line, the size of the arrowhead and the thickness (weight) of the line. You can also change the color of the line here. With each different autoshape object, you'll have similar but different options when you select the object and right click, bringing up the autoshape's format dialog box.

Let's go with a large arrowhead and a 2 pt. weight.

4) Select *2 pt* in the **weight:** command.
5) Select the largest arrowhead.
6) Now let's move the arrowhead so that it points at the top of the tower.
7) Place your pointer over the handle at the arrowhead.
8) Depress the left mouse button.
9) Keeping the button pressed, drag the arrowhead to the top of the tower.
10) Release the mouse button.
11) Move your pointer over the handle at the other end of the arrow.
12) Press the left mouse button.
13) Keeping the button pressed, drag the end of the arrow up into the picture, about halfway from the bottom and near the right side of the picture. (We have a reason.)
14) Release the mouse button.

Your picture should now look like this.

Figure 7-13 Repositioned Arrow

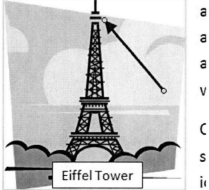

Add Informative Text Box

We've already added one text box. Now we're going to add another so that we can identify the height of the Eiffel Tower. In order to make the picture appear less crowded, we're going to use a smaller font. We've already shown you how to insert a text box and resize it, so we won't go over those details again. But, here are the steps:

1) Create a text box.
2) Type "986 ft." in the box.
3) Select the text in the box.
4) Click on the *Home* tab.
5) Select "**8**" as the font size in the *Font* group.
6) Resize the text box to fit the text in it.
7) Move the text box to the end of the arrow.

Your picture should now resemble ours. Congratulations. You've learned how to insert a picture and then enhance it to present information to the reader in a memorable way.

Figure 7-14 Completed Tower Picture

131

Summary

We hoped we've inspired you to learn more with text boxes and autoshape objects like arrows and to put them in your *Word* documents. You can do a lot with text boxes and autoshape objects, but explaining all of the options and commands would take a much longer book. If you're interested, we've supplied you with the basics. You can explore inserting other autoshape objects, moving them around in your document, and changing the object properties. Use *Help* to learn about different commands in the different format ribbons.

In this chapter, we've shown you how to insert a text box. We've typed text into the text box, resized the box, and moved the box around on the page.

We've inserted an arrow, although we've shown you how to insert other objects. We've also shown you how to insert pictures taken from your camera. One of the key points here is to know the folder location of your pictures. You could, of course, save them to your desktop.

With a simple arrow and a text box, you can turn a simple text document into a visually informative presentation. All you need to do is to become more familiar with these objects and integrate them into your work.

CHAPTER 8

Working with Tables

Introduction

Although the **Table** command is the only visible command in the *Tables* group, it is a powerful command. With it, you accomplish many features that require spacing on the page.

For example, if you're working solely with text, you can use the **tab** key to move your insertion point over to the right side of the page. But with a table, you can have areas of the table spread across your page, and you can put text or pictures in each.

Tables are also excellent tools to present information to the reader. Each column in a table, for example, could list the bills you pay each month. Or you could list inventory items in each room of your house. If you think about it, the month of a calendar is a table.

We'll show you how to insert tables, show you a few uses, and then it's up to your imagination and needs to come up with more ways to use your tables.

Insert a Table

Let's make this a project for home use. We'll point out how you could use it for a class paper as well, but we've found that, for some, knowledge acquired to produce a class paper can be quickly forgotten while knowledge acquired for the benefit of personal use can be more firmly ingrained.

And so let's assume for the moment that you want to make a list of chores for household members.

Let's get started.

1) Open a new document.
2) Type the name of your document, "Household Chores".
3) Press **enter** 3 (or so) times.
4) Click on the *Insert* tab.
5) Find the *Tables* group.

 The *Tables* group.

The *Insert Table* dialog box appears.

Figure 8-1

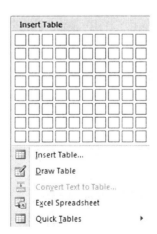

You could select, using your pointer and left mouse button, boxes to indicate how many columns and rows you want. Just move your pointer over the top left box, press the left mouse button, and move your pointer to the right and down until your table is the size you desire. Then release the mouse button.

Instead, we're going to use the **Insert Table ...** command.

> 6) Select **Insert Table ....**

Another *Insert Table* dialog box appears. We've entered the number of columns we want (**4**) and the number of rows (**7**).

Figure 8-2 Another Insert Table Dialog Box

> 7) Enter 4 for **Number of columns:**.
> 8) Enter 7 for **Number of rows:**.
> 9) Press **OK**.

 Click on the checkbox for *Remember dimensions for new tables* to have the same number of rows and columns for your next inserted table.

Your document should look similar to ours below. Notice that our table has lines for borders. Remember, when you insert a table, you might need to increase the number of rows by 1 if you want a header row (the same goes for columns). But don't worry. If you insert a table with too few rows (or columns), you can insert more later.

Figure 8-3 Household Chores table

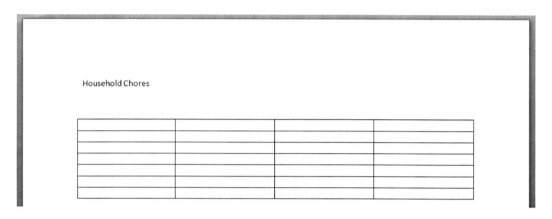

Also note that there are two new tabs. Because your table is selected, *Word* thinks you want to perform commands on it, so it gives you two tab options, *Design* and *Layout*.

Adding Text to Tables

Now we want to add our text to the table. Note that each "box" in our table is called a cell. You can move around from cell to cell by moving your pointer to the cell you want and clicking the mouse button. You can also use the arrow keys on your keyboard.

Type "Jeremy", "Jill", and "Jason" in the top row cells, skipping the first column. Type the days of the week, starting with "Monday" in the first column, skipping the first row. End with Saturday. (We're giving everyone Sunday off, so there'll be no Sunday chores.)

Select the first row by clicking and dragging your insertion point across it, or place your pointer in the left margin, beside the row, and left clicking. You'll know when the first row is selected because it will be highlighted.

Select the *Home* tab and click on **Center**. This centers the names in the cells.

Deselect the table by clicking elsewhere on the page.
Your table should now look like ours.

Figure 8-4 Table with Text

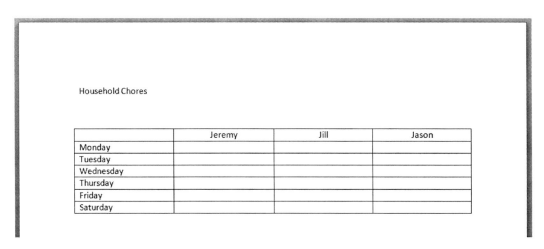

You can work with the text in a table just like you can work with text that exists anywhere else in your document. You simply have to select the text. Practice selecting a cell (and the text in it) by moving your pointer to the left side of a cell, near the border. The shape of your pointer might change, depending on your settings. When it is pointing at a cell, left click the mouse button. The cell becomes highlighted. Any text commands you choose will now affect the text within that selected cell.

Note that for a class paper, you could present other information in a table like this. For example, you could have a table titled *American Presidents by Century*. You could have in the first row, *1700s*, *1800s*, *1900s*, and *2000s*. In each column, you could then place the name of a president in a cell. Note that if your insertion point is in a cell, you can select the *Insert* tab, then select the **Picture** command to insert a picture into a cell in a table.

Let's take a step back for a moment and look at the two new ribbons that the **Insert Table** command has given you to work with. We'll come back to our *Household Chores* document later in this chapter.

Table Design Ribbon

The *Design* tab gives you three groups on the ribbon.

Figure 8-5 Design Ribbon for Tables

Click inside your table to put your insertion point in the table. The *Table* tabs become highlighted. Select the *Design* tab.

Now, move your pointer over the different *Table Styles* pictures of table in the center of the ribbon. As your pointer moves over each selection, the table in your document gives you a preview of what your table would look like if you select that style.

Notice that for our table, we have a "header" in the first row. This row highlights the names of the children. Our first column also has special significance in that it identifies days of the week.

Why do we point this out?

Because if you'll notice the *Table Style Options* group, there are different checkboxes that you can select. These will affect how the *Table Style* appears. You might, for example, want groups of two rows grouped together with different background colors.

Practice checking different checkboxes and seeing how this affects your table as you move your pointer over the *Table Style* selections.

There are, though, a few commands we want to highlight on the *Table Design* ribbon. Here are a couple of commands in the *Table Styles* group.

- **Shading** When you select a cell, a row, a column, or any number of cells, you can select the shading of those selected cells with this command.

- **Borders** When you select cells, or the entire table, you can select the borders for the selection. Sometimes, for example, you might not want a border on the top or bottom of a cell.

The *Draw Borders* group has a few more commands of interest.

- **Pen Color** This command selects the color of the borders of the cells.
- **Draw Border** You can draw additional cells or tables by selecting this command. After selecting it, click and drag to draw additional cells. Don't worry, *Word* squares the cells for you.
- **Eraser** You can erase cells or rows or columns (or an entire table!) with this command. After selecting it, click and drag to erase.

One other command in the *Draw Borders* group allows you to select the style of the lines for the borders in your table. This is the box with a line in it. Use the selection arrow to choose another line style. The other command allows you to select the point (pt.) size of your lines.

Table Layout Ribbon

Let's take a look at the *Layout* ribbon for tables. We'll be using some of these commands for our *Household Chores* document, so we'll leave this *Layout* tab selected as we move forward.

Figure 8-6 Layout Ribbon for Tables

We'll go through these groups one at a time, starting with the *Table* group on the left.

- **Select** Opens a dialog box that allows you to select different parts of the table. After cells are selected, you can perform commands on the selected cells.

- **View Gridlines** If you remove all of the borders in your table, you can still see where the borders are via gridlines. They display onscreen but do not show on the printed document. This command allows you to view or hide the gridlines.
- **Properties** Select different properties of the table here via a pop-up dialog box, including text wrapping, text alignment, borders and other table properties. These commands are similar to the text box commands discussed earlier.

The *Rows & Columns* group allows you to insert rows and columns. Select a row or column, and then select the appropriate command. You can also delete row and columns with the **Delete** command.

The *Merge* group allows you to merge multiple rows into one row and multiple columns into one column.

 Merging rows or columns can create formatting problems if there are different properties associated with each.

The *Cell Size* group allows you to choose the height and width of your selected cells. You can also choose to have the cells automatically conform to the size of the text in the cell with **Autofit**.

The *Alignment* group has picture commands to allow you to align the text to the left, middle, right, top, and bottom sides of the cell. There is also a **Cell Margins** command in this group. Select **Cell Margins** for a pop-up dialog box that allows you to choose the distance that your text appears from the border of the cell.

The *Data* group is for advanced users who want to fill their tables with numbers and perform math functions on them.

Household Chores

Let's go back to house *Household Chores* document. Select the first row and select **Bold** from the *Font* group under the *Home* tab. Type in chores such as 1) *Take* *garbage out*, 2) *Sweep floors*, and 3) *Wash dishes*. Select the cells with chores in them and select **Center** in the *Paragraph* group.

Your document should resemble ours.

Figure 8-7 Table with Chores

Household Chores

	Jeremy	Jill	Jason
Monday	Wash dishes	Take garbage out	Sweep floors
Tuesday	Sweep floors	Wash dishes	Take garbage out
Wednesday	Take garbage out	Sweep floors	Wash dishes
Thursday	Wash dishes	Take garbage out	Sweep floors
Friday	Sweep floors	Wash dishes	Take garbage out
Saturday	Take garbage out	Sweep floors	Wash dishes

If you wanted to make your table color coded, for example, you could assign a color to each chore. You could select each cell with *Wash dishes* in it and give that cell a red background. You could select blue for *Sweep floors* and green for *Take garbage out*.

For the final touches on our table, we're going to increase the cell size so that our table doesn't look so cramped. We'll also select a different right border on the first column to set apart the days of the week from the cells with chores.

10) Select the table by putting insertion point in it.
11) Click **Select**.
12) Click on **Select Table**.
13) Select the *Layout* tab.
14) Click on up arrow in **Cell Height** until **0.4"** is shown.
15) Click on **Align Center** in the *Alignment* group. (Center horizontally and vertically.)
16) Select the first column in the table.

17) Click on the *Design* tab.
18) Select **1½ pt.**
19) Select **Borders**. A dialog box appears.
20) Select **Right Border**.
21) Deselect the table.

Your table should look like ours.

Figure 8-8 Formatted Table with Chores

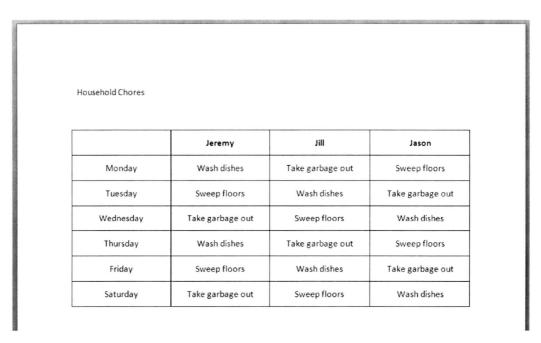

Household Chores

	Jeremy	Jill	Jason
Monday	Wash dishes	Take garbage out	Sweep floors
Tuesday	Sweep floors	Wash dishes	Take garbage out
Wednesday	Take garbage out	Sweep floors	Wash dishes
Thursday	Wash dishes	Take garbage out	Sweep floors
Friday	Sweep floors	Wash dishes	Take garbage out
Saturday	Take garbage out	Sweep floors	Wash dishes

Congratulations. You're on your way to becoming proficient with using tables. While you have your document open, select other commands to become more familiar with tables. Remember to save your document!

Summary

In this chapter, we learned how to insert tables into a document. We learned how to insert text into cells within a table.

We took our table and learned how to use the *Design* ribbon to change the appearance of our table. Additionally, we used the *Layout* ribbon to select other commands for our table, such as aligning text within the cells.

Cell borders can be different colors and constructed with thicker point sizes. Cells can be shaded with different colors to provide visual enhancement. Color codes can also be used by creative *Word* users to present more order to the information in their tables.

Remember, you can also insert pictures into your cells. If you create a table with two columns, you could insert pictures into the cells in the left column. In the right column, you could write descriptions of the pictures.

CHAPTER 9

Creating a Resume

Introduction

Many of the commands we'll talk about in this chapter have already been discussed in this book. This is a chapter that is going to bring many elements together. With some books on how to work with *Word*, you get nothing but descriptions of commands. Other books are more like exercise books, presenting problems and letting the reader figure out how to do it.

We're going to show you how to write a resume from scratch with *Microsoft Word 2007*. We'll show you briefly how to opt for a resume template, but that's not how we're going to make ours. While constructing our resume, you'll see how the commands we use affect the text.

Right away, we're going to start with a table, which we described in the last chapter. Our resume will have two columns. The left column will list the categories such as work experience and education. The column on the right will host the details.

Along the way, we'll work with *tabs* and **Font** commands.

We encourage you to work along with us while we construct a resume. If you're a student, this will be great practice for when you graduate and begin your job hunt. If you're currently looking for employment, you can improve your existing resume or come up with one that outshines the one you currently have. If you're employed ..., well, it never hurts to have an updated resume on file ... just in case.

New File

We're going to walk through this, step by step. So far in this book, we've encouraged you to repeat the process we used at the start, using the **Blank document** command. This time, we're going to show you a twist.

1) Click on the **Office** button.
2) Select **New**.

The *New Document* dialog box appears.

Figure 9-1 The New Document Dialog Box

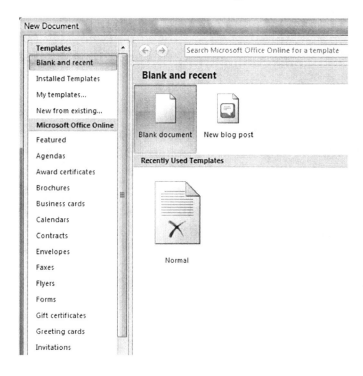

Creating a Resume

We have throughout this book instructed you to select **Blank document**. This time is different.

Use the scroll bar in the pane on the left to scroll down (alphabetically) through the document template groups.

 Browse through the templates, keeping in mind you might want to use one later. Templates can be great time savers. These documents open with formats and tables already established.

Keep scrolling until you find the **Resumes and CVs** template group. The choices you encounter may vary if you're connected to the Internet or not. Click on **Resumes** if that's your only choice.

Figure 9-2 Resumes and CVs Template

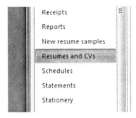

     3) Click on **Resumes and CVs**.

You'll notice that you're given a choice of resumes and CVs to choose from. In case you didn't know, a CV stands for *Curriculum Vitae*, which is basically a more detailed resume that lists published works and other items in a career.

Figure 9-3 Resumes and CVs Choices

 The first time you select a template, you may be given a choice only of *Resumes* in the templates pane. Select *Resumes* in this situation.

We're going to show you how you could select a resume template at this point. It will allow you to type in text to a pre-packaged document. This is fine as long as what you want to type in resembles what's in the template.

4) Click on **Basic resumes**.

You are give yet even more choice to choose from. This time, *Word* shows you previews of each document template.

Figure 9-4 Resume Template Choices

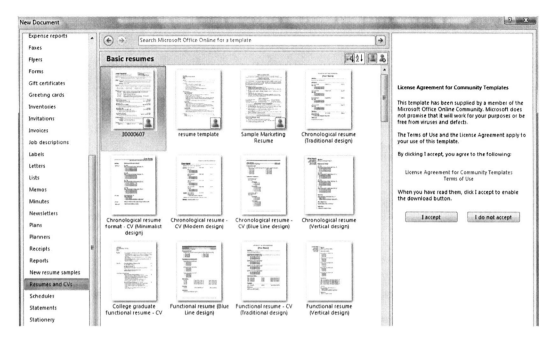

Note that some of the resume templates are supplied by Microsoft. Other resume templates are supplied by members of the Microsoft Office Online Community. If you select one of these templates (denoted by the avatars in the lower right corners of the previews), you will have to click on **I accept** for the licensing agreement.

5) Scroll through the templates by using the scroll bar.
6) Click on **Functional Resume (Minimalist design)**.

You should see a resume template in which you can enter your own name, address, and job-hunting skills.

Figure 9-5 Functional Resume Template

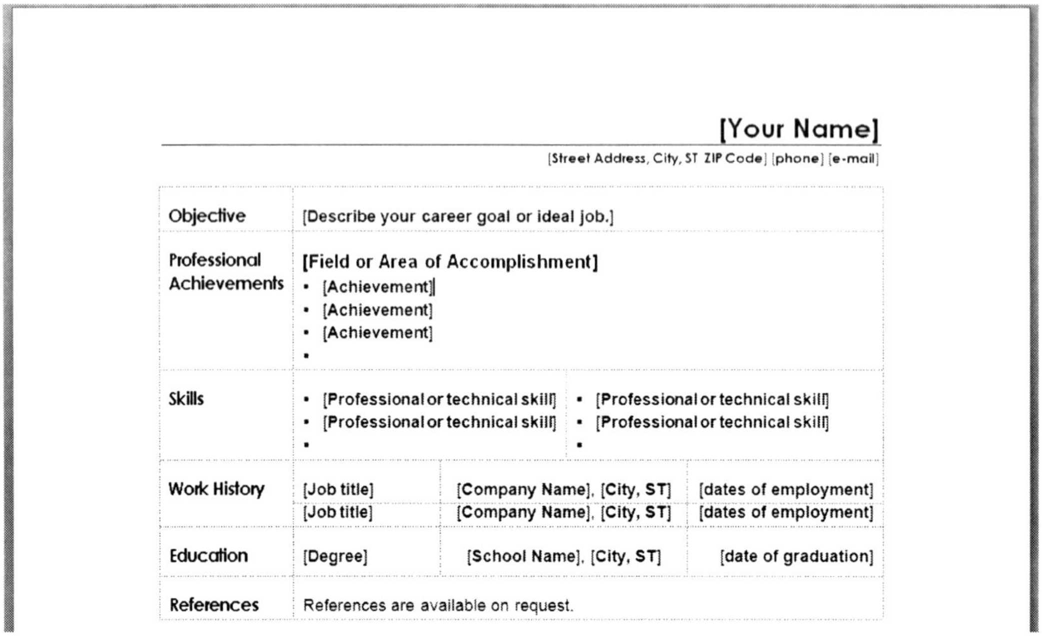

[Your Name]

[Street Address, City, ST ZIP Code] [phone] [e-mail]

Objective	[Describe your career goal or ideal job.]		
Professional Achievements	[Field or Area of Accomplishment] • [Achievement] • [Achievement] • [Achievement] •		
Skills	• [Professional or technical skill] • [Professional or technical skill] •	• [Professional or technical skill] • [Professional or technical skill] •	
Work History	[Job title]	[Company Name], [City, ST]	[dates of employment]
	[Job title]	[Company Name], [City, ST]	[dates of employment]
Education	[Degree]	[School Name], [City, ST]	[date of graduation]
References	References are available on request.		

We shorted the template to fit it in the picture, but you get the idea. Simply place your insertion point in the template and delete existing text and replace it with your own.

Remember to save it as a document and not as a template!

Create a Resume

By creating our own resume, we'll be able to go over many of the commands we've already covered in this book and cover a few more that we believe you'll find useful.

7) Click on the *Office* button.
8) Select **New**.
9) Click on **Blank document**.

10) Select **Create**.
11) Select the *Insert* tab.
12) Select **Table**.
13) Select **Insert Table ....**.
14) Select **2** columns and **6** rows.
15) Click on **OK**.

You should have a document that resembles ours.

Figure 9-6 New Document with Table

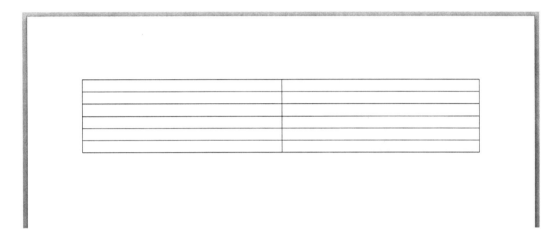

Name and Address

In a way, we're starting out with our own template. We have the cells on the page in which we're going to enter our resume. Keep in mind that there are hundreds, if not thousands, of ways to put your resume together. We're just going to put one together. Use your imagination to come up with your own design if you're so inclined.

1) Type your name in the first row, first column cell.
2) Click and drag to select the text in your name or simply select the cell.
3) Select the *Home* tab and change the font size to **20**.
4) Select **Bold** to put your name in bold text.
5) Select the first row, second column cell.

6) With the cell selected, place a left tab at the 4.5" mark on the ruler.
7) Place insertion point in the first row, first column cell.
8) Press **ctrl** and **tab** at the same time.

 When your insertion point is in a table, pressing tab moves your insertion point to the next cell. By pressing **ctrl** and **tab** at the same time, your insertion point moves to the tab we just established.

9) Type your street address.
10) Press **enter**.
11) Press **ctrl** and **tab** at the same time.
12) Type your city, state, and zip code.
13) Press **tab** to move your insertion point to the next cell.

While your insertion point is still in the first row, second column, you can add additional contact information such as your telephone number and email address. Simply press **enter** for a new line and then press **ctrl** and **tab** at the same.Your document should resemble ours. Don't worry; we'll get rid of the lines later. We wouldn't want them our resume, so we don't expect you'll want them in yours.

Figure 9-7 Contact Information in Resume

Jill or John Q. Public	123 Main Street AnyCity, AnyState 12345

Add Spacing

We don't want the *Objective* part of our resume, which will go in the second row, to crowd our contact information in the first row. We could insert some blank rows, or we could press enter several times to get our desired space. Instead, we're going to select a command that will place our second-row text one inch from the top border.

1) Select the entire second row in the table.
2) Select the *Home* tab.
3) Click on the **Launcher** (the arrow in the bottom right corner) of the *Paragraph* group.
4) Under the Spacing command selections, select **30 pt** for **Before:**.
5) Click on **OK**.
6) Place your insertion point in the second row, first column.
7) Type "Objective".
8) Press **tab** to move to the second column.
9) Type your career or job objective.

Your document should look like ours.

Figure 9-8 Objective in Resume

Jill or John Q. Public	123 Main Street AnyCity, AnyState 12345
Objective	To get a job working with widgets and gadgets.

Row Formatting

We have good spacing now between the body of our resume and our contact information. But we have a problem. The word "Objective" is far to the left of the page. It's difficult to connect the word with our actual typed-in objective. Also, it seems like having two columns of equal width isn't the correct way to proceed. After all, one column is going to have very few words, objective, education, etc, while the second column is going to have a lot of information.

It would be nice if we could make the first column more narrow, starting with the second row. And then align the first column text farther to the left.

Aha! We can do accomplish these tasks easily.

1) Select all of the rows except the first by pressing the left mouse button and dragging the pointer down, starting with the second row.
2) Move the pointer over the center table border indicator on the horizontal ruler. A helper text box may appear with the words "Move Table Column".

Figure 9-9 Column Border Adjust in Ruler

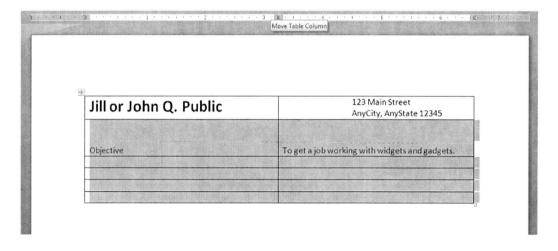

Press the mouse button and move the border to the left, aligning it with the period after "Q" in John Q. Public.

Figure 9-10 Narrowed First Column

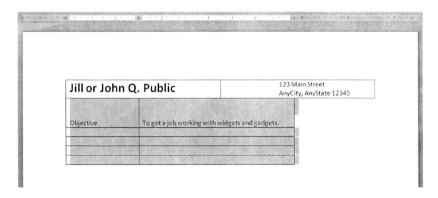

This is how we wanted the first column to look, but now the right border of our second column has also moved to the left.

Note that we have not deselected the rows yet. Rows 2 through row 6 are still selected. If you deselected them, click and drag to select the rows again because we're going to move the right border of those rows.

3) Move the cursor to the horizontal ruler and place it over the right border indicator. "Move Table Column" appears. If you cannot move the ruler border, position your cursor arrow over the right table border and drag it to the right until it is aligned and skip Step 4.

Figure 9-11 Selecting Right Border Control

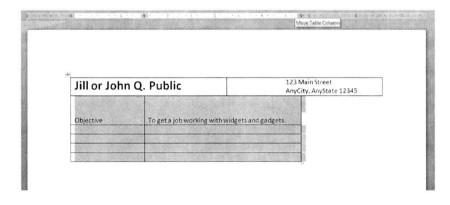

4) Press the left mouse button and move the border to the right until it is aligned with the right border of the first row.
5) Deselect the rows by clicking elsewhere on the page.

Your document should resemble ours.

Figure 9-12 Re-sized Columns

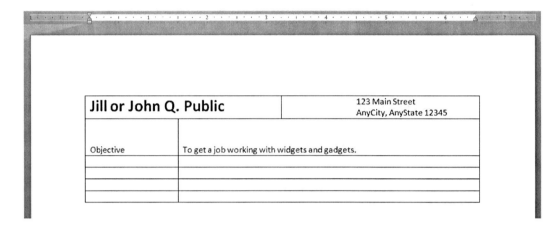

Jill or John Q. Public		123 Main Street AnyCity, AnyState 12345
Objective	To get a job working with widgets and gadgets.	

Our resume is starting to look good. If we can move the word "Objective" over to the right a little, we'll be happy with our alignment.

Looking ahead, we'll want the other words in our first column, such as "education" and "work experience", to have the same alignment, so we're going to select the first column, minus the cell in the first row. We'll have to make this selection by using our pointer, clicking in the second row, first column, dragging down the bottom of the first row, then releasing the mouse button. Then we'll add a tab to align the text to the right.

6) Select the cells in the first column, minus the first row cell.
7) Click on the tab select button at the left end of the horizontal ruler until the **right tab** appears.
8) Click on the ruler at the **1"** mark. Note this places a tab in the first column.

Your document should look like ours. Note the tab marker in the ruler.

Figure 9-13 Right Tab in First Column

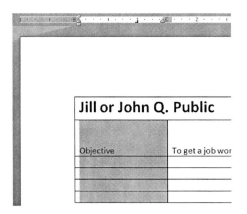

Okay, now we're ready to take advantage of the tab we just inserted.

9) Deselect the cells.
10) Place the insertion point at the start of the word "Objective" in the first column, second row.
11) Press **ctrl** and **tab** at the same time. (Remember, pressing tab in a table moves the insertion point to the next cell, and we want to align text to a tab setting. **Ctrl** and **tab** does this.)

Finally! Now your resume is in very good shape and should look like ours. The rest of the text will be easily typed in.

Figure 9-14 Aligned Column Text

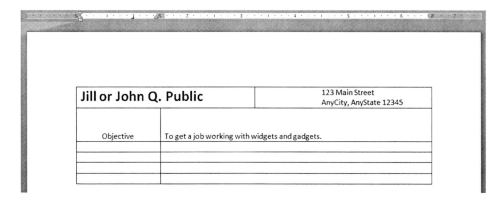

Now, we need to add some spacing between the rest of our rows, but we don't want the large gap that was needed beneath our contact information.

And so we'll go back to the *Paragraph* group after selecting our remaining rows.

Add More Spacing

As we prepare to write the rest of our resume, we want a little space between our *Objective* and our *Work Experience* sections.

How do we accomplish this?

The same way we added space before the *Objective* row. Only this time, we're going to select the four remaining rows and add space before each row. This will make our resume appear consistent and give it a smooth, professional feel. It will present another problem with spacing, but we'll show you how to correct the problem, and at the same time give you more experience with working with *Word*.

1) Select the bottom four rows by clicking and dragging.
2) Click on the *Home* tab.
3) Click on the *Paragraph* group's **Launcher**.
4) Select **18 pt** in the **Space before:** command window. You can click on the up and down arrows until **18** appears in the window or simply type **18** into the window. Click OK.

Your document should look like ours.

Figure 9-15 Increased Row Spacing

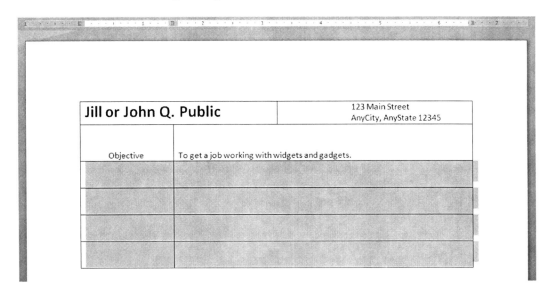

Note that our four rows are still selected. You can also notice that the border indicators are present in the ruler. Note the first column's right border indicator is showing up for the selected rows and *not* the first row.

Add Topic Text

Let's add the resume topics in the first column. Remember, we've already set a tab for these cells, and all of our topics will be right-aligned with *Objective*.

1) Click in the first cell below *Objective* to place your insertion point there.
2) Press **ctrl** and **tab** at the same time.
3) Type "Education".
4) Move your insertion point down one cell by clicking in the cell, pressing tab twice, or using the down arrow key.
5) Press **ctrl** and **tab** at the same time.
6) Type "Work Experience".
7) Move your insertion point down one cell by clicking in the cell, pressing tab twice, or using the down arrow key.
8) Press **ctrl** and **tab** at the same time.

9) Type "Computer Skills".
10) Move your insertion point down one cell by clicking in the cell, pressing tab twice, or using the down arrow key.
11) Press **ctrl** and **tab** at the same time.
12) Type "Hobbies".

Your document should look like ours.

Figure 9-16 Resume Topics Entered

Jill or John Q. Public	123 Main Street AnyCity, AnyState 12345
Objective	To get a job working with widgets and gadgets.
Education	
Work Experience	
Computer Skills	
Hobbies	

Entering Education Text

Now that our (neatly aligned) resume topics are all set, we need to enter the text for our topics. We're not going to go through line by line and instruct you what to type. But keep in mind that you can set tabs in each cell. You can press enter in each cell. You can add bulleted lists to each cell.

For the Education topic, we've added tabs and entered our college, city in which the college was located, the diploma/certificate earned, and the year it was earned. When we press enter, however, we see that we have a large gap between our college listings.

162

Figure 9-17 Education Text

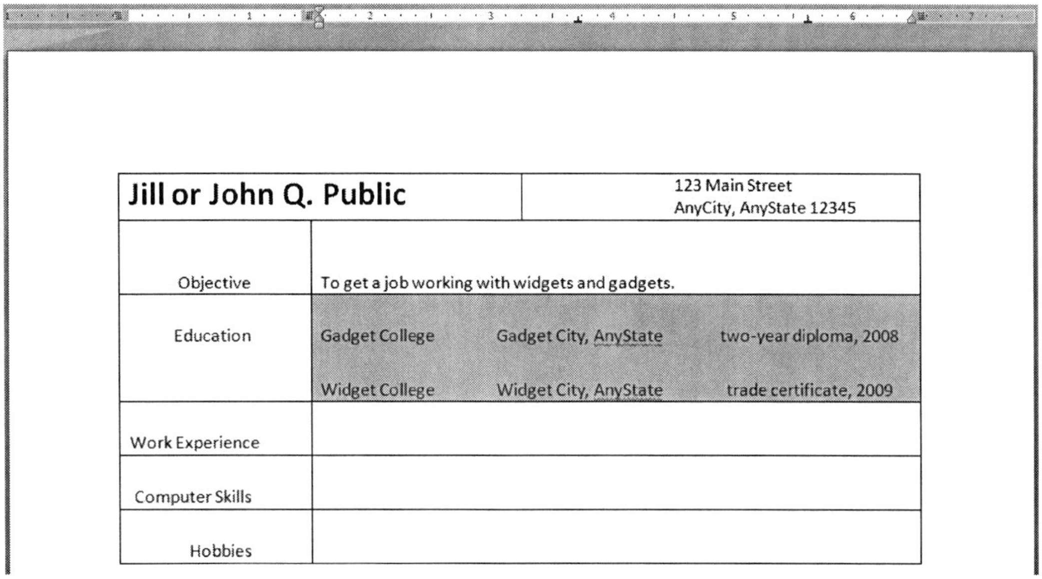

Jill or John Q. Public		123 Main Street AnyCity, AnyState 12345
Objective	To get a job working with widgets and gadgets.	
Education	Gadget College Gadget City, AnyState two-year diploma, 2008 Widget College Widget City, AnyState trade certificate, 2009	
Work Experience		
Computer Skills		
Hobbies		

We need to correct the spacing in this cell.

1) Select the second line of text in the cell.
2) Click on the *Home* tab.
3) Click on the *Paragraph* group's **Launcher**.
4) Select **6 pt** in the **Space before:** command window. You can click on the up and down arrows until **6** appears in the window or simply type **6** into the window.

Congratulations. Your second line of text in the Education cell moves up. We use this trick of paragraph spacing often with our work, especially with one-page documents that we're creating for a single use. Check to see if your document looks like ours.

Figure 9-18 Properly Spaced Education Text

Jill or John Q. Public		123 Main Street AnyCity, AnyState 12345	
Objective	To get a job working with widgets and gadgets.		
Education	Gadget College	Gadget City, AnyState	two-year diploma, 2008
	Widget College	Widget City, AnyState	trade certificate, 2009
Work Experience			
Computer Skills			
Hobbies			

Let's move on to *Work Experience* and *Computer Skills*. Let's put bulleted lists in these. After we enter the text and get the spacing right, we'll move to our last row, Hobbies, and then get rid of those lines.

We hope that during this process you're beginning to see how to view a document page and imagine where text can (or should) go on the page, and then by using your imagination, you can come up with *Word* commands to allow you to achieve your goals.

Text for Work Experience and Computer Skills

We're only going to enter three items each for work experience and computer skills. Your resume might have less or more items. But we are going to ask that for one of your items, use enough text that it will use text wrapping within the cell; that is, the sentence will run up against the right border of the cell and will automatically wrap around to the next line at the left border of the cell. For us, we'll do this with the first item in our Work Experience cell. We'll combine the steps below for each cell.

Position your insertion point in the *Work Experience* or *Computer Skills* cell.

1) Type in text for your first item. For the *Work Experience* cell, try to think of enough text that it text wraps (that is, it is longer that the width of the cell).
2) Press **enter**.
3) Type in text for your second item.
4) Press **enter**.
5) Type in text for your third item.

Your document should resemble ours. We want you to note that the spacing in the first item in the *Work Experience* cell looks good. That's because we have placed extra spacing (via the *Paragraph* group's **Launcher**) before each paragraph (a new paragraph starts when enter is pressed) and not before each line of text.

Figure 9-19 Work Experience and Computer Skills Text

Jill or John Q. Public		123 Main Street AnyCity, AnyState 12345
Objective	To get a job working with widgets and gadgets.	
Education	Gadget College Gadget City, AnyState two-year diploma, 2008 Widget College Widget City, AnyState trade certificate, 2009	
Work Experience	Worked as an associated widget maker and Widget Maker Enterprises, including big widgets and small widgets. 2007 - present Assembled gadgets on the assembly line at Gadget Industries. 2006-2007 Designed widgets and gadgets for W&G Online for an internship. summer 2008	
Computer Skills	Extensive knowledge of Widget Computer Design application Partial experience with Gadget On The Web designs Working knowledge of document writing applications	
Hobbies		

165

Let's correct the spacing between the second and third items in the Work Experience cell.

6) Select the second and third lines in the Work Experience cell.
7) Click on the Home tab.
8) Click on the *Paragraph* group's **Launcher**.
9) Select **6 pt** in the **Space before:** command window. You can click on the up and down arrows until **6** appears in the window or simply type **6** into the window.
10) Deselect the text.

Look at our document and see how the spacing has changed in the Work Experience cell. You can change the spacing to whatever looks best to you.

Figure 9-20 Work Experience Text with Corrected Spacing

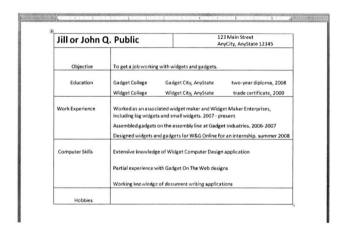

Let's make our *Computers Skills* text a bulleted list.

Computer Skills Text

You will notice as we make the text in our Computer Skills cell a bulleted list, the text will become spaced correctly. That's because bulleted lists have their own spacing rules. That's fine. It saves us from having to change spacing between lines.

1) Select the text in the Computer Skills cell.
2) Click on the *Home* tab.
3) Select **Bullets**. (Choose style of bulleted list if necessary.)

Your document should now look like ours. Note the spacing of the bullets.

Figure 9-21 Bulleted Computer Skills Cell

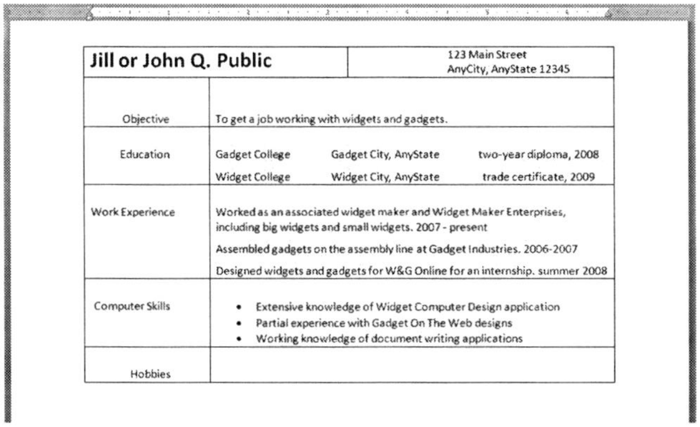

Hobbies Text

There are many different types of resumes. Some people like resumes that add a personal touch, especially if the personal items support a professional demeanor or add to the possible skill sets that an employer might be looking for.

1) Place your insertion point in the *Hobbies* cell.
2) Type three hobbies or personal interests, pressing enter after each hobby or interest.
3) Select the three lines of text in the *Hobbies* cell.
4) Click on the *Home* tab.
5) Select **Bullets**. (Choose style of bulleted list if necessary.)
6) Deselect the text.

Your resume should look like ours. Note how the spacing appears good, but we still have those lines, which we definitely do not want in our final copy.

Figure 9-22 Bulleted Hobbies Cell

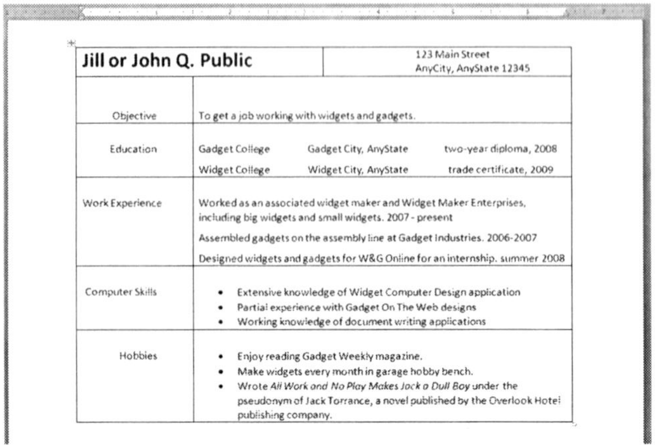

Jill or John Q. Public	123 Main Street AnyCity, AnyState 12345
Objective	To get a job working with widgets and gadgets.
Education	Gadget College Gadget City, AnyState two-year diploma, 2008 Widget College Widget City, AnyState trade certificate, 2009
Work Experience	Worked as an associated widget maker and Widget Maker Enterprises, including big widgets and small widgets. 2007 - present Assembled gadgets on the assembly line at Gadget Industries. 2006-2007 Designed widgets and gadgets for W&G Online for an internship. summer 2008
Computer Skills	• Extensive knowledge of Widget Computer Design application • Partial experience with Gadget On The Web designs • Working knowledge of document writing applications
Hobbies	• Enjoy reading Gadget Weekly magazine. • Make widgets every month in garage hobby bench. • Wrote *All Work and No Play Makes Jack a Dull Boy* under the pseudonym of Jack Torrance, a novel published by the Overlook Hotel publishing company.

Removing Lines

Let's remove the lines from our resume. First we're going to remove the lines that would print if we printed our resume. Then we'll remove the gridlines, which don't print, so you can see what your final document will look like when you send it via email or print.

1) Place insertion point in the table (anywhere).
2) Click on the *Layout* tab in *Table Tools*.
3) Click on **Properties**.
4) Click on the **Borders and Shading ...** button.
5) Click on **None** in **Setting**.
6) Click on **OK** twice.
7) Deselect the table by clicking elsewhere.

Your resume should look like ours. The lines have been replaced by dotted lines, which are called gridlines so you can see the location of the table cells.

Figure 9-23 Lines Removed from Resume

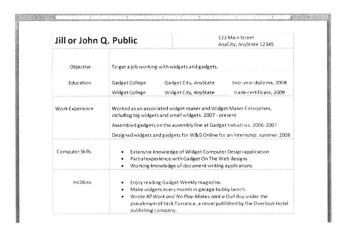

Remove Dotted Lines (Gridlines)

Now all we have to do is remove the gridlines.

1) Place your insertion point in the table (anywhere).
2) Click on the *Layout* tab in *Table Tools*.
3) Click on **Select** in the Table group.
4) Click on **Select Table**.
5) Click on **Properties** in the Table group.
6) Click on **Borders and Shading ...**.
7) Select **None** in **Setting:**. Click OK twice.
8) Click on **View Gridlines** (if your gridlines are present).

Your resume should now look like ours. Congratulations. You've come a long way in working with *Word*. Your resume is proof.

Figure 9-24 Resume with No Lines

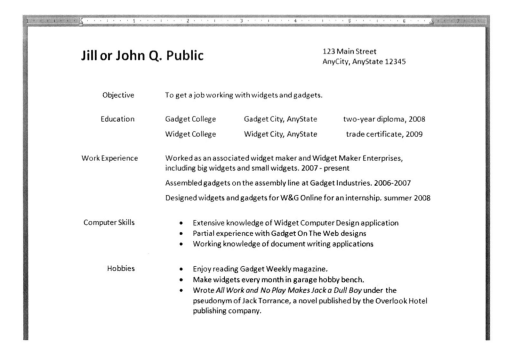

Summary

In this chapter, we brought together many of the previous lessons in order to construct a resume.

We used text formatting commands, such as Bold. We showed you how to resize your text.

Tabs were used to position text in the table cells. We used a right-justify tab in order to place text at the right end of a cell.

In summary, this chapter brought together the lessons learned in this book. We hope that you can use the knowledge in order to benefit you directly, whether by a resume that gets you a job or a letter that gets you admitted into the college of your choice.

CHAPTER 10

Odds and Ends

Introduction

We wanted to take the opportunity in this last chapter to cover some topics that have not yet appeared in this book. There are several reasons for this, but it's not because we don't use the topics in this chapter. In fact, some of these topics cover commands that we most often use in *Word 2007*.

We will cover our favorite topics, our most-used commands, and other bits of trivia with Word. Then we'll talk about what we hope you take away from a book like this, and what we hope we've been able to teach you during the passing of these pages.

So, let's get started on this last chapter.

Zoom

With computer monitors coming in so many sizes and people having eyesight that may or may not be impeccable, it is nice to have a command to magnify the document on which you're working. Using Zoom won't change the way the document appears when it is printed. The only change is how the document appears on the monitor. Think of it as taking out your magnifying glass and looking at your document.

Everything becomes …, well, magnified.

Let's see how it works.

1) Open a new document.
2) Type some text.

Here's what our text looks like.

Figure 10-1 Default Magnification

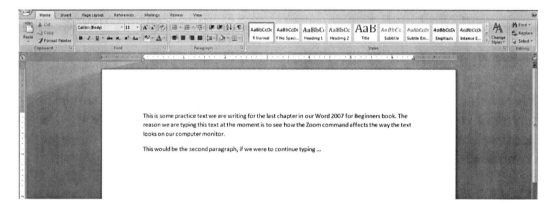

3) Select the *View* tab.
4) Click on **Zoom**.

Note there are different settings you can choose. Try out different ones to see what effect they have. We like using **Page Width** because it gives us a little magnification while being able to see much of the page onscreen.

5) Click on the **Page Width** radio button.
6) Click **OK**.

Your document should look like ours.

Figure 10-2 Page Width Magnification

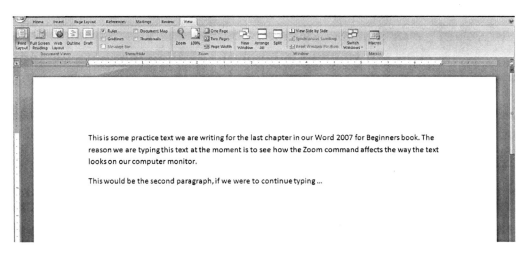

Let's see what 200% magnification looks like.

7) Select **Zoom**.
8) Click on **200%** radio button.
9) Click **OK**.

This is what our document looks like.

Figure 10-3 200% Magnification

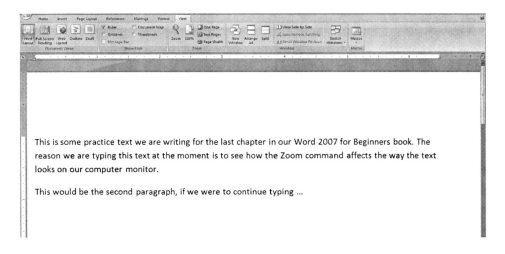

We hope you find a Zoom setting that suits both your needs and your eyesight.

Keyboard Shortcuts

We would like to go over a few keyboard shortcuts.

A keyboard shortcut is a command that takes effect because of the keys that you press. It's called a shortcut because you could select the command by going to the ribbon, finding the command, and clicking on it.

But sometimes pressing keys is quicker, especially if you use the command a lot. We'll give you four of the keyboard shortcuts that we use daily. And we rarely use any others. That's not to say others aren't useful; they're just not useful to us.

ctrl + c	**Copy** Highlight text (or a picture or any object) and press **ctrl** and **c** at the same time. Word copies the selection to the clipboard.
ctrl + x	**Cut** This command deletes the selection (text or picture) and places it on the clipboard.
ctrl + v	**Paste** Whether you have cut or copied text (or a picture), this command pastes it into the document at the insertion point.
ctrl + z	**Undo** This command undoes your last command.

Insert Symbol

Sometimes there are symbols we want to put into our document that are not on the keyboard. For example, we might want to insert a copyright symbol, or ©. Or we might need a small circle to indicate temperate, the degree symbol, as in 75 °F.

In order to insert these symbols, and any other available symbols, we simply have to know where to look. Symbols like the copyright symbol are more commonly used, so to find the degree symbol we have to look a little farther. Use the same Word document that we used for the **Zoom** command (or open a new document).

    1) Click on the *Insert* tab.

    2) Click on **Symbol** in the *Symbols* group.

You'll see a choice of commonly used symbols you can select from the pop-up dialog box.

Figure 10-4 2 Commonly Used Symbols

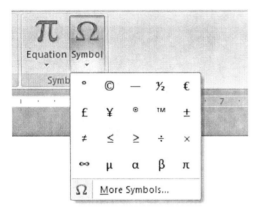

    3) Click on the *copyright symbol*.

The copyright symbol inserts automatically. Now move your insertion point to where you want to insert the degree symbol. Then follow these steps.

    4) Click on the *Insert* tab.
    5) Click on **Symbol** in the *Symbols* group.
    6) Click on **More Symbols ….**.

A new dialog box will open with a scroll bar. You can scroll down the choices to find the symbol you want. For us, the degree symbol is near the top of the choices so we don't have to do any scrolling. Note our highlighted box in the following picture. "DEGREE SIGN" appears in text near the bottom left of the dialog box to tell us what we've selected.

Figure 10-5 More Symbols

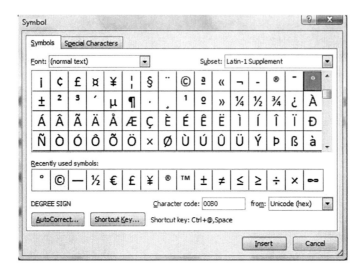

7) Find the *degree* symbol and select it by clicking on it.
8) Click on **Insert**.
9) Click on **Close**.

You can see how we've inserted these symbols into our document below. Look through the symbol choices to see what's available.

Figure 10-6 Inserted Copyright and Degree Symbols

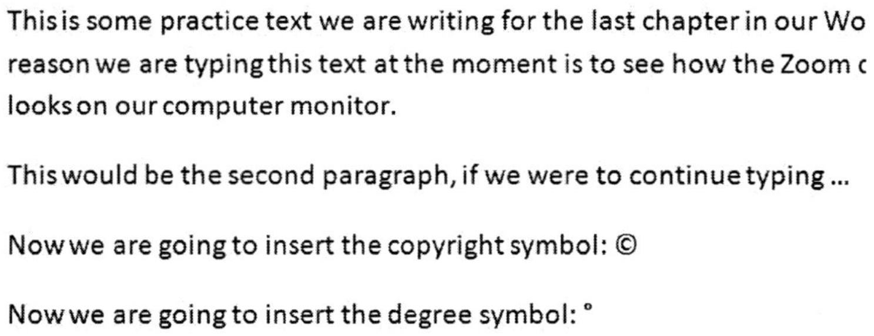

> This is some practice text we are writing for the last chapter in our Wo
> reason we are typing this text at the moment is to see how the Zoom c
> looks on our computer monitor.
>
> This would be the second paragraph, if we were to continue typing ...
>
> Now we are going to insert the copyright symbol: ©
>
> Now we are going to insert the degree symbol: °

As a final note for this section, you might have noticed when you clicked on

More Symbols, there was an additional tab selection available. This tab was titled *Special Characters*. We just wanted to point this out to you in case you wish to insert *M dashes* or other symbols such as a *non-breaking hyphen* (the hyphen and all of the hyphenated word(s) will text wrap to the next line instead of text wrapping at the hyphen).

Figure 10-7 Special Characters

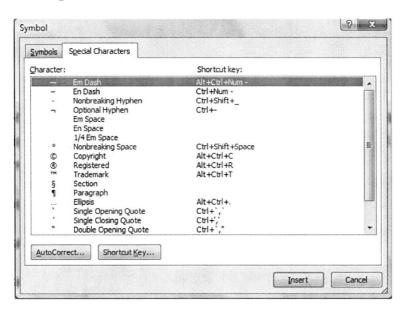

So, now that you're well acquainted with inserting symbols and special characters, let's move on to *WordArt*.

WordArt

WordArt is a fancy name for an application that *Word* used to present your text in a graphical image. This could be an excellent method to create a flyer. By the way, there are templates that you can use for fliers, also.

For now, we're just going to show you how to make a Family Reunion announcement with *WordArt*.

1) Open a new document.
2) Click on the *Insert* tab.

 Whenever you create a new document, consider hitting **enter** a few times before starting your typing. This gives you lines above your work in case you want to add text later. You can always delete these lines later.

3) Click on **WordArt** in the *Text* group.

You will see a dialog box open. This box shows you the different ways your text will appear when you type it in.

Figure 10-8 WordArt Style Choices

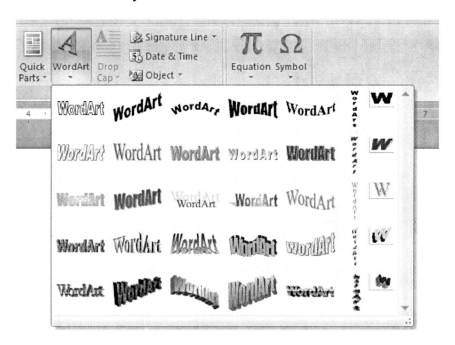

4) Select a style of *WordArt* by clicking on one of the choices.

An *Edit WordArt Text* box appears. This is the box in which you type your text.

Figure 10-9 Enter WordArt Text

5) Type your text.
6) Click **OK**.

Here is what our document looks like after performing our *WordArt* commands. (We centered it by selecting **Center** in the *Paragraph* group under the *Home* tab.)

Figure 10-10 WordArt in Document

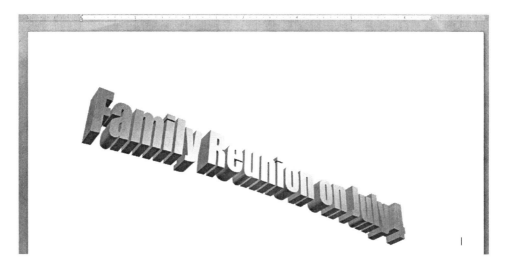

Remember that your *WordArt* text is like a picture. You can select it, which will show you the handles. Click and drag on a handle and you can make your *WordArt* bigger or smaller. You can also perform any of the other commands on a *WordArt* object as you can any other object or picture.

Conclusion

We showed you some odds and ends in this last chapter of our book. We pointed out some keyboard shortcuts, a few ways to liven up your documents by using *WordArt*, how to view your documents more closely via the **Zoom** command, and how to insert symbols and special characters.

We hope that this book has helped you to learn the basics of *Microsoft Word 2007*. It is a powerful program for word processing, and sometimes there seems to be too many commands. We want to make a document and wonder, where do we start?

This book, we hope, has given you that starting point.

Throughout, we have encouraged you to explore the commands and options that Word provides. We believe that is by playing with *Word*, you'll get to know it better, and indeed become proficient at using it.

Remember to use *Word Help* if you get stuck. Or try starting over with a new document. By practicing, that is, by using *Word* frequently, you'll get to try new commands and find the ones you need to get your document the way you want it.

Good luck and best wishes. We enjoy using *Word 2007*, and we hope you'll come to enjoy it, too.

Index

H

header, 72, 85, 99, 100, 101, 102, 104, 105, 106, 107, 108, 109, 110, 111, 112, 137, 140
height, 121, 127, 131, 142, 143
help, 17, 19, 26, 32, 49, 50, 59, 60, 63, 64, 70, 76, 85, 86, 88, 89, 92, 99, 100, 107, 115, 119, 125, 132, 182
high school, 56

I

icons, 18, 21, 24, 26, 92
illustration, 115, 116, 128
indent, 43, 45, 46, 52, 57, 60, 65, 66, 67, 68, 69, 70, 80
insert page, 112
instructions, 51, 116
italics, 19, 21, 35, 42, 101

K

keyboard, shortcuts, 39, 176, 182

L

layout, 20, 25, 63, 78, 79, 80, 118, 138, 141, 143, 145, 168, 169
left justify, 56
line spacing, 43, 44, 45, 53, 55-60

M

margins, 26, 44, 60, 63, 64, 65, 80, 110, 142
menu, 73, 84, 85, 90, 94
Microsoft, 17, 18, 19, 20, 21, 24, 29, 36, 49, 50, 51, 57, 83, 84, 86, 90, 94, 102, 118, 147, 151, 182
mini toolbar, 39, 40, 41, 46

LaVergne, TN USA
20 November 2009
164848LV00008B/1/P